LESSONS IN TEACHING READING COMPREHENSION IN PRIMARY SCHOOLS

LESSONS IN TEACHING READING COMPREHENSION IN PRIMARY SCHOOLS

SUZANNE HORTON, LOUISE BEATTIE AND BRANWEN BINGLE

Los Angeles | London | New Delhi
Singapore | Washington DC

Learning Matters
An imprint of SAGE Publications Ltd
1 Oliver's Yard
55 City Road
London EC1Y 1SP

SAGE Publications Inc.
2455 Teller Road
Thousand Oaks, California 91320

SAGE Publications India Pvt Ltd
B 1/I 1 Mohan Cooperative Industrial Area
Mathura Road
New Delhi 110 044

SAGE Publications Asia-Pacific Pte Ltd
3 Church Street
#10-04 Samsung Hub
Singapore 049483

Editor: Amy Thornton
Development editor: Geoff Barker
Production controller: Chris Marke
Project management: Swales & Willis Ltd,
Exeter, Devon
Marketing manager: Lorna Patkai
Cover design: Wendy Scott
Typeset by: C&M Digitals (P) Ltd, Chennai, India
Printed by: CPI Group (UK) Ltd, Croydon, CR0 4YY

Library of Congress Control Number: 2015937414

British Library Cataloguing in Publication Data

A catalogue record for this book is available from
the British Library

ISBN 978-1-4739-1613-5
ISBN 978-1-4739-1614-2 (pbk)

Contents

The authors

Suzanne Horton has spent 20 years working in primary schools and has had experience teaching all year groups across the primary age phase. She worked as an Advanced Skills Teacher (AST) and as a Local Authority Literacy consultant while maintaining a teaching responsibility in school. She is currently subject leader for primary English at the University of Worcester and teaches on a range of postgraduate and undergraduate modules. She has recently been involved in the Lifelong Readers Project in co-operation with a number of European partners, funded with support from the European Commission.

Louise Beattie has spent over 20 years working in secondary schools as a teacher of English. She has worked as subject leader, whole school literacy co-ordinator, local authority adviser and more recently English tutor at the University of Worcester for the secondary PGCE course. She has experience of teaching Key Stages 3 and 4, Post-16 and has taught literacy in Years 5 and 6. She has been a member of the National Association for the Teaching of English drama committee 2004–09 and is a committee member for the National Association of Advisers in English.

Branwen Bingle moved from primary teaching into initial teacher education in 2008. Her career path to date has been anything but straightforward: she has been a supply teacher and support assistant for Service Children's Education; a basic skills tutor working with adults in the military; a private day nursery teacher working with 3- and 4-year-olds; a secondary English teacher working across Key Stages 3 and 4, including the teaching of GCSE English; and a subject leader for English in two Worcestershire Middle schools. In addition to her lecturing role, Branwen is currently working on doctoral research into children's literature and its potential influence on professional identity construction/aspiration.

Acknowledgements

Every effort has been made to trace the copyright holders and to obtain their permission for the use of copyright material. The publisher and author will gladly receive any information enabling them to rectify any error or omission in subsequent editions.

We would like to dedicate this book to our families for their unwavering support and patience.

For Suzanne – Alex and Emma: my little readers.

For Louise – Mum, Dad, Paul, Tilly and George.

For Branwen – In memory of my mother Mervynne Payne: the most inspiring teacher of reading I have ever known.

Chapter 1

What is reading?

Learning outcomes

The way we communicate without being present, through a myriad of symbols on a blank surface, would seem to be a uniquely human trait. While production of the signs and symbols is miraculous enough, being able to access their meaning connects us to people and places we may not come across in our daily lives. This chapter explores what is meant by the term *reading* as an activity that enables the communication circle to be completed.

This chapter will allow you to achieve the following outcomes:

- understand what reading is and what it entails;
- understand different theories of learning to read.

Teachers' Standards

Working through this chapter will help you meet the following standard:

3. Demonstrate good subject and curriculum knowledge.

Making sense of reading

> 'Twas brillig and the slithy toves
>
> Did gyre and gimble in the wabe
>
> ('Jabberwocky' by Lewis Carroll)

In order to access the extract from Lewis Carroll's poem, several things have to happen simultaneously. You have to recognise the alphabetical system being used (try reading a translation using Chinese characters or in Arabic to see how different codes look); you have to have an understanding of the grapheme–phoneme correspondence; you have to be familiar with written grammatical structures; and you have to be experienced enough to know that not everything you read will make sense the first time you decode it. Indeed, decoding alone does not a reader make! However, a good reader will not give up at the nonsense words: a good reader, one who enjoys reading, will return to the text time and again, playing with the words in his or her mind, turning them over and savouring them until they get a sense of what brillig might represent, or how to gyre and gimble with the same abandon as the slithy toves.

Debates around the teaching of reading, and the primacy of certain approaches, are not new. Meek (1988) decried the way *reading experts ... decontextualize reading in order to describe it*, pointing out the absurdity of removing the text from the process, and at the same time acknowledging that reading, in and of itself, is a field of study. But what constitutes reading?

Activity

Try to remember the first book you ever read, or at least a book from your early childhood.

- What alphabetic code was used? Were words involved at all?
- Was it fiction or non-fiction? How did the genre affect the presentation of the text?
- Did it have features other than written text, e.g. illustrations or diagrams?

What skills, knowledge and understanding enabled you to read it?

Understanding reading: Influential approaches

Reading, according to Cremin *et al.* (2014, p5) *is often characterised as a personal solitary experience conducted in privacy, yet even when readers read alone, the act of reading remains profoundly social.* Many linguists have studied the process of learning to read and Lambirth (2011) identifies three approaches that have been particularly influential in UK educational policy development around the teaching of reading. These are Cognitive-Psychological, Psycholinguistic and Sociocultural approaches: each is underpinned by ideological and theoretical paradigms, and each is characterised by its effect on pedagogical models.

The Cognitive-Psychological approach

The Cognitive-Psychological approach, or CPA, focuses on the way an experienced reader instructs emergent readers in a systematic way to ensure reading competence. CPA favours grapho-phonic cues in the early stages of reading. For the purposes of teaching reading it is important that grapheme–phoneme correspondence (GPC) is established first and foremost before readers attempt individual comprehension of the written word. It is a bottom-up approach: readers start from the way that sounds are represented on the page and build up to reading whole words, sentences and texts through achievable steps. This is in contrast, although not opposite, to the Psycholinguistic 'top-down' model (see Figure 1.1).

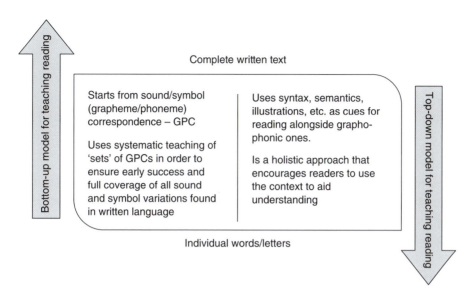

Figure 1.1 Models for teaching reading based on CPA and Psycholinguistic approaches

Proponents of CPA advocate this approach as they feel that top-down models which utilise contextual cues can mask reading difficulties, i.e. the child is able to guess what word will come next, rather than knowing how to work out the words on the page (even when unfamiliar) using the graphemes linked to sounds in a way that is phonetically plausible. This has become particularly influential in UK educational policy since the publication of the *Independent Review of the Teaching of Early Reading* (Rose 2006) and its support for systematic synthetic phonics and re-introduction of Gough and Tunmer's *Simple View of Reading* (see Chapter 2 for an explanation). While we as authors are accepting of the Simple View of Reading (SVoR) as a helpful model, it is with a word of caution: the SVoR can encourage professionals to disengage with the complexity of each of the axes (word recognition and language comprehension) in an attempt to reduce reading to manageable chunks, but it is only by recognising that very complexity in relation to each axis, and equipping yourself with the subject knowledge needed to teach both, that you will be able to help children overcome barriers to reading.

Activity

The focus of this book is reading comprehension and thus it is not the place to unpick or explain the phonics debate. However, it is still useful to identify your own subject knowledge regarding grapheme–phoneme correspondence as it is one of the cueing strategies used in both CPA and Psycholinguistic approaches. Use the following questions to audit your knowledge.

- How many sounds (phonemes) are generally thought to be used in the spoken English language?
- How many graphemes (not necessarily individual letters) are used to represent the phonemes?

(Continued)

(Continued)

- A long /o/ sound can be written in several different ways, for example <u>oh</u>; h<u>o</u>pe; l<u>oa</u>f; kn<u>ow</u>; d<u>o</u>n't. List five different graphemes used to represent a long /a/ sound.
- What are *blending* and *segmenting*?
- What are the key differences between *synthetic* and *analytic* phonics?

CPA has many advocates, but it is still contested and debated as an approach to reading. While CPA focuses on the technical skills needed to successfully master reading, other approaches view all language, written and spoken, as innate to human development. It is within this tradition that we find the Psycholinguistic approach.

The Psycholinguistic approach

Psycholinguists hold the opinion that human beings have a predisposition to learn how to communicate and that the development of written language is not fundamentally different to the development of oral language. Rather than being a hindrance or 'mask' for poor performance, utilisation of symbolic representation is a necessary part of the communication process. Most importantly within psycholinguistics, literacy is not a school-based activity: it is part of life, and many literacy experiences happen well before formal schooling begins.

Ken Goodman, probably the most well-known self-confessed psycholinguist, cites many seminal influences on the development of his model for the development of reading, most notably perhaps *Chomsky's concept of language competence underlying language performance* (Goodman, 2005, p6). Better known as the Whole Language approach, Goodman's 'top-down' model sees reading as a process which pulls together three cueing strategies: grapho-phonic, syntactic and semantic (see Figure 1.2).

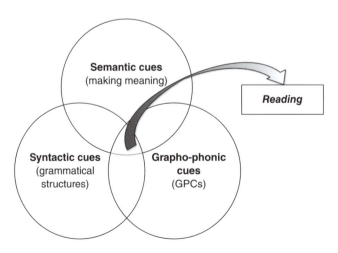

Figure 1.2 Cueing strategies for reading (Psycholinguistic model)

The Psycholinguistic approach does not view reading as the mere application of a set of technical skills: it is more part of the innate way that humans are able to make meaning for each other. In this way, reading becomes a meaningful, and thus enjoyable, aspect of human behaviour, although Goodman was keen to distance this approach from Behaviourist theories. The role of the teacher in the Whole Language approach is not to *change* behaviour; it is to *enable* through the facilitation of meaningful reading experiences. Far from being redundant, the teacher or expert reader provides real books, models effective reading and shares literacy experiences to help extend and develop learners' competencies. Assessment is ongoing and continuous, achieved through observation of children's practices, and the reading environment is adjusted accordingly to meet the readers' needs.

The Sociocultural approach

Psycholinguistic and Cognitive-Psychological approaches have been heavily advocated (and criticised!) in the so-called reading wars of the last 30 years (see Chapter 2), with CPA gaining significant ground within UK educational policy. However, in the popular press there is still a regular link made between underachievement in literacy and social deprivation. If reading is merely a set of technical skills which teachers can instruct learners to acquire, then surely, in any education system that entitles all children to a school place, illiteracy should have been eradicated long ago.

The issue for some researchers is that literacy is a sociocultural event and thus cannot be addressed through technical instruction in the absence of a supporting sociocultural environment. As Lambirth (2011, p34) reminds us, *school literacy is also not neutral or autonomous*; rather, it is based on a particular ideological position and reinforced through social and cultural practices. The same can be said of the home and all other environments experienced by the child. Thus, within the Sociocultural perspective, communication happens through a series of events, and social and cultural factors not only affect how we read these communications, they often dictate our familiarity and expertise regarding the mode of communication. This means reading is not restricted to written texts, which is what differentiates it from the Psycholinguistic approach (despite many overlaps in ideology).

In Sociocultural classrooms a range of literacies are recognised and valued, for example digital, visual, etc. Thus it could be conceptualised as similar to the Psycholinguistic model but with the addition of non-alphabetic codes and cues (see Figure 1.3).

The value of recognising the sociocultural influences on reading development is often overlooked. Goouch and Lambirth (2011, p6) state that the *assumption made in government statistics is that there is a homogenous literacy culture to which we all belong*, and the implication is that this prevalent culture is based on a narrow set of parameters. This would seem to be borne out by the recent revisions to the National Curriculum within England, which has removed previous references to multicultural and multimodal learning objectives in favour of phonics 'first and fast', followed by the explicit teaching of books and authors children *might not choose themselves. Pupils should also have opportunities to exercise choice in selecting books and be taught how to do so* (DfE, 2013, p37). This guidance

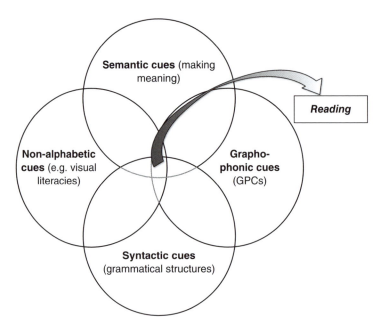

Figure 1.3 Cueing strategies for reading (Sociocultural model)

is actually easier to follow if one relates it to sociocultural aspects of learning to read, whether that was the intention or not; however, in order to do this effectively the teacher needs to understand the full extent of the literacy practices being undertaken outside of the school environment along with the confidence and the subject knowledge to build upon these in the development of new expertise.

Activity

Think about the many ways we communicate and list up to five. Try to identify the knowledge and/or strategies we need in order to make meaning from the method of communication: one way has been listed for you in Table 1.1.

Table 1.1   Types of communication and knowledge/strategies required

Method of communication	Knowledge/strategies
Email	Understanding of alphabetic code; familiarity with technological convention (no capital letters in address; use of @ symbol); understanding of icons and their use in electronic communication (e.g. ✉🖫), etc ...

Learning outcomes review

When teaching reading it is useful to be aware of the wider research, and the three approaches presented here are recognisable in current educational policy and debate. However, it might be more beneficial to choose pragmatism over one or other of the approaches discussed. Borrowing from the different theoretical bases to suit children's needs is preferable to blind adherence to one or other approach. But be aware: it is only possible to make informed decisions about the best way to teach reading if you first become properly informed.

Points to consider are as follows.

- There are different linguistic models that theorise reading development: which aspects do you think have already influenced your teaching?
- How might these different models affect or change your classroom practice?

Further reading

Chomsky, N (1955) Logical syntax and semantics. *Language*, 31 (1): 36–45.

An early journal article by linguist Noam Chomsky which critiques the idea that syntax is separate to semantics in linguistics, and in particular focuses on the inability of artificial models of syntax to *increase our awareness of the subtleties of actual language* (p45). Particularly useful if you wish to study linguistics at Master's level and beyond.

Goodman, K (1996) *On Reading: A Common-Sense Look at the Nature of Language and the Science of Reading.* Portsmouth, NH: Heinemann.

A seminal text for those who want to teach reading using Psycholinguistic approaches. It outlines Goodman's approach to reading as a means to make sense out of print.

Goouch, K and Lambirth, A (2011) *Teaching Early Reading and Phonics: Creative Approaches to Early Literacy.* London: Sage.

This book provides a useful overview of pedagogical approaches to teaching reading in its widest sense. It also outlines ways to create effective reading environments and provides practical as well as theoretical guidance.

Janks, H (2009) *Literacy and Power.* London: Routledge.

Part of the *Language, Culture and Teaching* series. Interesting for those interested in sociocultural perspectives, this text focuses on critical literacy.

References

Cremin, T, Mottram, M, Collins, FM, Powell, S and Safford, K (2014) *Building Communities of Engaged Readers: Reading for Pleasure.* London: Routledge.

Department for Education (DfE) (2013) *The National Curriculum in England: Framework Document.* London: DfE.

Goodman, K (2005) Making sense of written language: a lifelong journey. *Journal of Literacy Research*, 37 (1): 1–24.

Gough, PB and Tunmer, WE (1986) Decoding, reading, and reading disability. *Remedial and Special Education*, 7: 6–10.

Lambirth, A (2011) Reading, in Cox, R (ed.) *Primary English Teaching: An Introduction to Language, Literacy and Learning*. London: Sage.

Meek, M (1988) *How Texts Teach What Readers Learn*. Stroud: Thimble Press.

Rose, J (2006) *Independent Review of the Teaching of Early Reading*. Nottingham: Department for Education and Skills (DfES).

Chapter 2

Reading in context

Learning outcomes

Our practice in teaching children to read is heavily influenced by a comprehensive body of theoretical knowledge and research which has been discussed and debated for many years. Government policy also dictates, to a certain extent, the way in which reading should be taught within the classroom. This chapter reviews the historical perspectives, provides an overview of key research findings and explores the pedagogical approaches that determine effective teaching of reading comprehension within the statutory framework introduced in September 2014.

This chapter will allow you to achieve the following outcomes:

- develop an overview of the historical background on teaching reading;
- understand the theoretical perspectives that underpin the teaching of reading comprehension;
- develop an understanding of the pedagogies associated with the teaching of effective reading comprehension.

Teachers' Standards

Working through this chapter will help you meet the following standards:

1. Set high expectations which inspire, motivate and challenge pupils:

   - Establish a safe and stimulating environment for pupils, rooted in mutual respect.
   - Set goals that stretch and challenge pupils of all backgrounds, abilities and dispositions.

2. Promote good progress and outcomes by pupils:

   - Be aware of pupils' capabilities and their prior knowledge, and plan teaching to build on these.
   - Demonstrate knowledge and understanding of how pupils learn and how this impacts on teaching.

3. Demonstrate good subject and curriculum knowledge:

- Have a secure knowledge of the relevant subject(s) and curriculum areas, foster and maintain pupils' interest in the subject, and address misunderstandings.
- Demonstrate a critical understanding of developments in the subject and curriculum areas, and promote the value of scholarship.
- Demonstrate an understanding of and take responsibility for promoting high standards of literacy, articulacy and the correct use of standard English, whatever the teacher's specialist subject.

Introduction

The only important thing in a book is the meaning that it has for you.

(W. Somerset Maugham)

Reading comprehension is at the heart of the reading process for it allows individuals to make sense of the text within their own experiences. This, in itself, is problematic for teachers in terms of assessing understanding because it is likely that each reader will have a slightly different interpretation of the text based on what they bring to the text themselves. Therefore, is it truly possible to define comprehension as deriving meaning from a text? Comprehension is an interactive process and is developed through active engagement with the text. It requires children to look closely at texts in order to derive meaning and to make decisions based on what has been stated or inferred. According to Guppy and Hughes (1999), comprehension takes the form of three levels, each of which necessitates attention by the reader.

- Reading the lines – the reader derives meaning from what is explicitly stated in the text.

- Reading between the lines – the reader has to infer meaning based on what the author implies.

- Reading beyond the lines – the reader evaluates the text based on the reactions and the feelings that the author has evoked.

By applying the above skills, children will be drawing meaning from the text and through discussion, dialogue and debate, these meanings can be re-shaped and re-contextualised so that readers not only make sense for themselves but can explain this to others. In this way, we are able to assess individuals' levels of comprehension. Throughout this chapter, we will draw upon the historical and theoretical background that has shaped the teaching of reading over the past four decades while addressing the requirements of the current statutory framework within which we teach. This will enable you, as the reader, to reflect upon current thinking and situate the teaching of reading within your own practice.

Activity

Consider the following extract from *Ulysses* by James Joyce:

> *Her antiquity in preceding and surviving succeeding tellurian generations: her nocturnal predominance: her satellitic dependence: her luminary reflection: her constancy under all her phases, rising and setting by her appointed times, waxing and waning: the forced invariability of her aspect: her indeterminate response to inaffirmative interrogation: her potency over effluent and refluent waters: her power to enamour, to mortify, to invest with beauty, to render insane, to incite to and aid delinquency: the tranquil inscrutability of her visage: the terribility of her isolated dominant resplendent propinquity: her omens of tempest and of calm: the stimulation of her light, her motion and her presence: the admonition of her craters, her arid seas, her silence: her splendour, when visible: her attraction, when invisible.*

> (Joyce, 1922)

What meanings have you derived from the text? What do you think Joyce is describing? What strategies did you employ in order to make sense of this piece of text?

You may find it difficult, at first, to understand exactly what Joyce was writing about. Jot down your ideas and the strategies employed and then compare with a colleague. Do you have the same understanding? Are you able to clarify meaning through discussion? How did you re-shape your own ideas in light of what someone else said?

Strategies for making sense of the text may have included the following:

- Re-reading the text in order to gain a 'feel' for the writing.
- Attention to punctuation in order to understand syntax.
- Word association – terribility, antiquity.
- Prior knowledge of the moon and words most commonly associated with this.
- Morphological awareness – *how meaningful word parts, morphemes, are arranged to create words* (Templeton, 2012, p101)
- Knowledge of affixes – inaffirmative.
- Vocabulary – nocturnal, satellitic.
- Background knowledge that you have gained through life experience – would everyone make the connection between the moon and the effect it has upon the 'effluent and refluent' waters?

Consider the implications that this may have for your own classroom practice when teaching reading comprehension.

The reading wars

Best practice in teaching children to read has long been a bone of contention, not only in the UK, but throughout the world; the 'reading wars' have raged long and hard during this time. The publication in America in 1955 of Rudolph Flesch's book, *Why Johnny Can't Read*, attacked the 'whole word' theorists and suggested a return to an emphasis on phonetic knowledge in order to address falling literacy standards in American schools. This polarised debate as to how best to teach reading continues to dominate current thinking in the UK, particularly as the teaching of phonics is a statutory requirement of the National Curriculum for English. The place of phonics in teaching children to read as opposed to teaching children to make meaning of texts is at the heart of this debate, although it is widely recognised that the majority of educators agree that a balanced approach is most effective (Levy, 2011). Indeed, Rose recognised that although phonics is essential in learning to read, it is *not the whole picture, of what it takes to become a fluent reader* (Rose, 2006, p16).

The historical context

Forty years ago, the Bullock Report (DES, 1975) concluded that there was *no one method, medium, approach, device, or philosophy that holds the key to the process of learning to read* (DES, 1975, p77). This far-reaching report was in response to perceived declines in literacy levels in schools. It addressed the teaching of all aspects of English in schools and made a series of recommendations for improving practice, although it did little to dispel the controversy surrounding the methods by which reading was taught. However, within the key recommendations, it recognised the importance of schools developing a comprehensive and systematic approach to reading in order to secure reading competence. Together with a more rigorous approach to training pre-service and existing teachers in the teaching of reading, reading was afforded a renewed rigour in terms of methods and pedagogical approaches.

The Cox Report (DES, 1989), which formed the basis of the 1988 National Curriculum for English, reiterated this view of teaching reading by stating that *teachers should recognise that reading is a complex but unitary process and not a set of discrete skills which can be taught separately in turn and, ultimately, bolted together* (DES, 1989, p21). It advocated teaching reading for meaning alongside decoding and recognised the reader as an 'active participant' in the process. Although the National Curriculum of 1988 has been criticised in terms of its prescriptive content, once again, reading was highlighted as having a pivotal role in driving up standards of literacy.

The Searchlights Model gained credence with the introduction of the National Literacy Strategy Framework for Teaching (DfEE, 1998), which consisted of a number of reading strategies that combined top-down and bottom-up approaches that children could employ to read a text. The Searchlights Model advocated an approach whereby children were encouraged to apply a range of strategies or 'cues' simultaneously. By drawing upon a diverse range of strategies, readers would not have to rely upon one but use as many of these strategies as required in order to make sense of the text (see Figure 2.1). The model itself had no basis in educational research (Stuart, 2005) but attempted to align the different approaches to teaching reading.

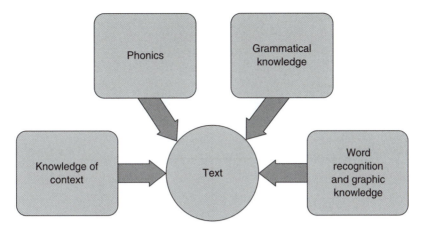

Figure 2.1 Searchlights Model

This model had its fair share of critics, most notably OFSTED, which stated:

> the 'searchlights' model proposed in the framework has not been effective enough in
> terms of illustrating where the intensity of the 'searchlights' should fall at the different
> stages of learning to read. While the full range of strategies is used by fluent readers,
> beginning readers need to learn how to decode effortlessly, using their knowledge of
> letter-sound correspondences and the skills of blending sounds together.

(OFSTED, 2002, para 58)

Once again, the National Literacy Strategy was condemned as having failed our
children in teaching them to read effectively. This led to a subsequent turnaround in
government policy and an independent report into the teaching of early reading was
commissioned, led by Sir Jim Rose. Rose (2006) concluded that synthetic phonics
should be the prime approach in teaching early reading based on evidence from the
Clackmannanshire study (Johnston and Watson, 2005). However, it should be noted
at this point that while word recognition for children in this study had increased
significantly, the reading comprehension test reported an average gain of 3.5 months
above chronological age, which has since led to much speculation as to the effectiveness
of phonics 'fast and first' in teaching children to *read* (Ellis, 2007; Wyse and Styles,
2007). As authors of a book on reading comprehension, this is a significant factor in
examining how word recognition and language comprehension should form part of an
interrelated process if we are to successfully teach reading.

The Simple View of Reading

The Rose Review (Rose, 2006) drew upon a conceptual model developed 20 years
earlier, known as the Simple View of Reading (Gough and Tunmer, 1986), which
consists of two key components: word recognition and language comprehension (see
Figure 2.2). Both have to be demonstrated in order to be a successful reader.

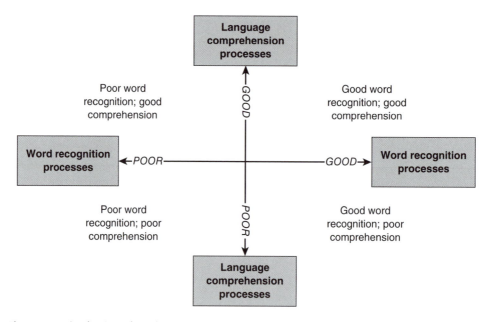

Figure 2.2 Simple View of Reading model

According to this model, learning to read involves recognising written words and understanding what these mean. While the decoding element is time limited, language comprehension is a lifelong process and children will continue to build upon this throughout their time in school and beyond. Both sets of processes are necessary if children are to become successful readers; however, neither is sufficient in itself. If a child is able to decode words correctly but has difficulty understanding the text, they will require further support in this area and vice versa.

Activity

Consider the following case study.

Emma was in Year 3. She was a confident and articulate child who enjoyed listening to stories and was able to make predictions, summarise the story and discuss character and plot in detail. However, when asked to read, she was hesitant and found it difficult to blend phonemes in order to decode successfully. Furthermore, when spelling words phonetically, she often omitted the vowels – 'bucket' was represented as 'bkt and 'sand' as 'snd'. Eventually, Emma was diagnosed as having a slight hearing impairment which had impacted upon her acquisition of phonetic knowledge as she had been unable to hear certain phonemes clearly. Evidently, Emma had good language comprehension but poor word recognition and a variety of intervention strategies were put in place to address her needs.

Think of a child that reads to you. Do they sit in one of the quadrants in Figure 2.2 above?

If so, consider next steps – how might you support this child in terms of their reading?

So, what now?

Taking into account the Simple View of Reading, the National Curriculum for English (DfE, 2013) separates reading into two areas: word reading and comprehension and sets out the age-related requirements for each within the statutory framework. Both appear to have equal weighting and one without the other will not secure success. The National Curriculum recognises *that it is essential that teaching focuses on developing pupils' competence in both dimensions; different kinds of teaching are needed for each* (DfE, 2013, p4) if children are to become fluent and informed readers as they make the transition to secondary school. There are many excellent textbooks for teachers that explore phonics in terms of subject knowledge and classroom practice; therefore, we make no apologies that this book explores the teaching of comprehension skills. As you explore the chapters on effective lessons, you will be able to draw upon best practice that has been informed by research and policy which will allow you to ensure children fulfil their potential as lifelong readers.

Classroom approaches to teaching reading

Shared reading

The shared reading model as a means of teacher and children reading together was developed by Holdaway (1979). It is an interactive process whereby children join in with the text as it is read by the teacher, typically from a 'big book' or an enlarged text visible on the interactive whiteboard. This provides an ideal opportunity for the teacher to explicitly teach reading strategies through effective modelling. The teacher is able to support children to become critical readers and reflect upon authorial intent so as to develop a deeper understanding of the text. In this way, we are encouraging children to engage in purposeful reading and become reflective, independent readers. There are many benefits to this approach.

- Children are able to access texts that they may not necessarily be able to read independently, thus allowing them to demonstrate comprehension skills on a different level.

- Children will have opportunities to contribute to the activity through reading with the teacher or contributing to the discussion that follows.

- It meets the individual needs of all readers, as those that find the text challenging can be supported through the process by the shared aspect of the activity.

- Focuses on reading skills.

- Increases vocabulary.

- Addresses reading comprehension.

- Allows children access to more complex texts.

If employed appropriately, shared reading provides an ideal opportunity for focused interactions between teacher and learner through the use of tailored questioning and effective modelling. Through careful management of this whole-class strategy, assessment of children's understanding of a text can take place. Consider how you would ensure that all children are active participants in this activity so that valuable learning takes place.

Guided reading

Guided reading is the perfect activity to engage children in constructive discussions about what they are reading through focused questions and tailored interventions. It encourages children to develop as active and independent readers, extending opportunities provided by shared reading.

Originally developed in New Zealand as a means of teaching groups of early readers (Simpson, 1966), guided reading was considered a successful strategy because it encouraged individuals to read for meaning and engage in thoughtful, reflective conversations with others; a key pedagogy explored in many of the chapters in this book.

Table 2.1 Guided reading session in five parts

	Supporting adult	Children
Book introduction or recap	Share the focus of the session and ensure all children are aware of the learning objective. Ask questions to activate prior knowledge. What do the children know already? Are they familiar with the subject content? What experiences have they had that they might bring to the text? Are they aware of other stories by the same author?	This allows children time to discuss the book and reflect upon the content. They are able to formulate questions and make links to prior experience and knowledge. They may be able to clarify unfamiliar vocabulary and concepts.
Strategy check	Remind children of the repertoire of strategies they can use for making sense of the text. Observe spelling patterns and make links to phonics to ensure successful decoding. Explore any unfamiliar words in terms of meaning.	Employ word recognition skills in order to decode unfamiliar words. Have the confidence to tackle challenging words.
Independent reading	Pose a question that the children will be able to discuss, having accessed the first few pages. Observe and 'listen in' as children read quietly to themselves, intervening at the point of need. Praise children for the use of specific strategies.	Children read independently and quietly at their own pace. The question posed by the teacher ensures that each child will be engaged in purposeful reading.
Return to the text	Revisit and review the questions posed at the start. Ask for contributions from each member of the group and facilitate an informed discussion using open-ended questions. Assess understanding.	This allows each group member to contribute to a facilitated discussion in order to articulate their views and deepen their understanding of the text. Children are able to respond, justifying their opinions and evaluating the overall impact of the text.
Next steps	This may take place outside of the guided reading session. Activities are provided to ensure children interact purposefully with the text.	Children are engaged in text-related activities designed to extend and further understand the text.

In today's classrooms, guided reading is teacher-led, with a clear focus, and usually takes place with groups of six to eight children of similar reading ability. All children have a copy of the same text, which is usually pitched at a level slightly above the children's's ability to ensure that reading instruction takes place. It is a time for teaching reading; not listening to individuals decode several pages!

The session is usually divided into five parts outlined in Table 2.1.

Guided reading is a powerful tool for assessment, allowing you, as the teacher, time to ask and respond to questions. From observations made during this time, you will be able to tailor subsequent sessions to meet the needs of individual readers and provide appropriate challenge and support through choice of text, use of questioning and implementation of guided activities to extend thinking. However, it is important to remember that all children learn in different ways and at different rates; therefore, continuous assessment will often necessitate moves within and between groups for some children. It is this flexibility of approach that is crucial to ensure that children move on in their learning, for as OFSTED point out in their report, *Reading by Six, teachers must exercise professional judgements about organising teaching groups to provide optimum conditions for learning* (OFSTED, 2010, p38). By ensuring fluid groups for guided reading, teaching can be closely matched to children's learning to ensure a level of challenge for all.

Book circles and book talk

Book circles can build effectively upon guided reading sessions and provide opportunities for groups of children to share and discuss their reading with an adult as they are more heavily focused on developing comprehension. Careful planning and organisation will ensure that all participants have opportunities to engage in a rich discussion that actively enhances their understanding of the text. Aidan Chambers explores this through his 'Tell Me' framework (Chambers, 2011), whereby children are encouraged to enter into conversations about the books they are reading. The use of 'tell me' instead of a more interrogative approach consisting of 'why?' and 'how do you know?' allows for the session to follow a child-led approach rather than a teacher-directed question and answer session. Some of the most successful book circles in school involve children sitting together at snack time, gossiping about the books they have read.

However, to ensure book circles are purposeful and effectively engage learners, it is important that the facilitating adult *guides* and *supports* the discussion. Posing thought-provoking questions that allow children to bring their own experiences, knowledge and values to the text will inevitably lead to greater comprehension. The expectation that children will build upon each other's contributions, co-constructing meaning through negotiation and justification of opinions, should underpin these discussions.

Individual reading

The practice of individual reading in the classroom has declined somewhat as guided reading has replaced it as the main vehicle through which children are heard to read. According to some (Browne, 2009), individual reading was seen to be ineffective as it was a rushed process relying on over-correction rather than the development of reading comprehension skills. However, if we think of these times as reading conferences in which a child and an adult have the opportunity to engage in one-to-one conversations about their individual reading book, we are more likely to acknowledge the benefits. The extent to which the adult scaffolds the learning is dictated by the individual learner, therefore providing a personalised approach to the teaching of reading. The teacher can attend to any misconceptions at the point of need and respond to misunderstandings by encouraging the reader to draw upon their repertoire of reading strategies. It is an ideal time to develop understanding of a text through high-quality discussion and allows both formative and summative assessment to take place. The place of individual reading (or reading conferences) necessitates careful organisation of resources and staff to ensure meaningful learning takes place and next steps are clearly identified for each child. This is not always easy in a busy classroom; therefore, it is imperative that you consider the implications of this in your own classroom and draw upon the views and opinions of others to ensure its success.

A final thought

As teachers, we seek to ensure that our children are fully equipped with the necessary tools to access a wide variety of texts. This chapter is concerned with the best way in which to teach reading comprehension while satisfying the requirements of the National Curriculum. We believe that reading is possibly the most important skill of all, empowering learners to embrace all aspects of the curriculum. The development of readers who are enthusiastic, motivated and knowledgeable about texts is at the heart of this book, and in the following chapters we have outlined some of the ways in which you can encourage your children to develop the lifelong reading habit.

Learning outcomes review

The best way to teach children to read has been greatly debated over the years and by now you should have a more comprehensive overview of how research has informed current teaching methods, allowing you to reflect upon how this may impact upon your own class-room practice. You will have a greater understanding of how to teach elements of reading comprehension through the implementation of successful teaching strategies that encourage and promote purposeful book talk.

Further reading

Chambers, A (2011) *Tell Me: Children, Reading and Talk.* Stroud: Thimble Press.

Together with his website, **www.aidanchambers.co.uk/index.htm**, this book offers an excellent framework which can be adapted and implemented in the classroom to develop 'book talk', which can, in turn, promote informative discussions and encourage dialogic talk.

Department for Children, Schools and Families (DCSF) (2008) *Effective Teaching of Inference Skills for Reading: Literature Review.* Nottingham, DCSF.

This document presents an evidence-based rationale for teaching inference and deduction skills.

Department for Education and Skills (DfES) (2003) *Guided Reading: Supporting Transition from Key Stage 1 to Key Stage 2.* Nottingham: DfES.

This document, although out of print, can be accessed via **www.teachfind.com/national-strategies/guided-reading-supporting-transition-key-stage-1-key-stage-2**. It provides a complete overview for teaching guided reading with advice for school leaders and class teachers.

References

Browne, A (2009) *Developing Language and Literacy 3–8.* London: Sage.

Chambers, A (2011) *Tell Me: Children, Reading and Talk.* Stroud: Thimble Press.

Department for Education (DfE) (2013) *The National Curriculum in England: Framework Document.* London: DfE.

Department for Education and Employment (DfEE) (1998) *National Literacy Strategy: Framework for Teaching.* London: DfEE.

Department for Education and Science (DES) (1975) *A Language for Life: The Bullock Report.* HMSO: London.

Department for Education and Science (DES) (1989) *English for Ages 5–16: The Cox Report.* HMSO: London.

Ellis, S (2007) Policy and research: lessons from the Clackmannanshire synthetic phonics initiative. *Journal of Early Childhood*, 7 (3): 281–97.

Flesch, R (1955) *Why Johnny Can't Read*, cited in Soler J and Openshaw, R (eds.) (2006) *Literacy Crises and Reading Policies: Children Still Can't Read!* London: Routledge.

Gough, PB and Tunmer, WE (1986) Decoding, reading, and reading disability. *Remedial and Special Education*, 7: 6–10.

Guppy, P and Hughes, M (1999) *The Development of Independent Reading.* Buckingham: OUP.

Holdaway, D (1979) *The Foundations of Literacy.* Sydney: Ashton Scholastic Research.

Johnston, R and Watson, J (2005) A seven year study of the effects of synthetic phonics teaching on reading and spelling attainment. *Insight 17*. Edinburgh: SEED.

Joyce, J (1992) *Ulysses.* St Ives: Penguin Fiction (first published 1922).

Levy, R (2011) *Young Children Reading at Home and at School.* London: Sage.

OFSTED (2002) *The National Literacy Strategy: The First Four Years, 1998–2002.* London: OFSTED.

OFSTED (2010) *Reading by Six.* Manchester: OFSTED.

Rose, J (2006) *Independent Review of the Teaching of Early Reading.* Nottingham: DfES.

Simpson, M (1966) *Suggestions for Teaching Teading in Infant Classes.* London: Methuen Educational.

Stuart, Dr M (2005) *Select Committee on Education and Skills: Memorandum Submitted by Dr Morag Stuart* [online]. Available at: **www.publications.parliament.uk/pa/cm200405/cmselect/cmeduski/121/4111503.htm**

Templeton, S (2012) Teaching and learning morphology: a reflection on generative vocabulary instruction. *Journal of Education*, 192 (2/3): 101–7.

Wyse, D and Styles, M (2007) Synthetic phonics and the teaching of reading: the debate surrounding England's Rose Report. *Literacy*, 41 (1): 35–42.

Chapter 3

Year 1: Using questioning with picture books

Learning outcomes

This chapter explores how you can develop language comprehension and reading comprehension in the classroom using picture books to promote and encourage discussion and dialogue.

This chapter will allow you to achieve the following outcomes:

- know how language comprehension can aid understanding of texts, including visual and multimodal forms;
- develop an understanding of how questioning can be used to extend thinking;
- have a greater awareness of the ways in which you can support this through classroom activities.

Teachers' Standards

Working through this chapter will help you meet the following standards.

3. Demonstrate good subject and curriculum knowledge.
4. Plan and teach well-structured lessons.
5. Adapt teaching to respond to the strengths and needs of all pupils.
6. Make accurate and productive use of assessment.

Links to the National Curriculum

Year 1 programme of study

READING – Comprehension
Pupils should be taught to:

- develop pleasure in reading, motivation to read, vocabulary and understanding by:

  - ✓ listening to and discussing a wide range of poems, stories and non-fiction at a level beyond that at which they can read independently
  - ✓ being encouraged to link what they read or hear read to their own experiences

   ✓ becoming very familiar with key stories, fairy stories and traditional tales, retelling them and considering their particular characteristics

   ✓ recognising and joining in with predictable phrases

   ✓ learning to appreciate rhymes and poems, and to recite some by heart

   ✓ discussing word meanings, linking new meanings to those already known

- understand both the books they can already read accurately and fluently and those they listen to by:

   ✓ drawing on what they already know or on background information and vocabulary provided by the teacher

   ✓ checking that the text makes sense to them as they read and correcting inaccurate reading

   ✓ discussing the significance of the title and events

   ✓ making inferences on the basis of what is being said and done

   ✓ predicting what might happen on the basis of what has been read so far

- participate in discussion about what is read to them, taking turns and listening to what others say
- explain clearly their understanding of what is read to them.

(DfE, 2013)

Key focus: Building on language comprehension

Activity

Firstly, what do you understand by the term 'language comprehension'? List any key words that help you to define comprehension.

This will help you to situate comprehension as a taught skill and may also have prompted you to remember how you were taught to comprehend texts. You may have no recollection of being taught explicit comprehension strategies or you may recall reading endless short passages and answering questions about the text. The teaching of language comprehension will be explored in further detail as you read through this chapter.

For children to comprehend a text, they have to be able to understand the language associated with it. Time needs to be spent developing children's oral language skills so that they are able to deepen their understanding. Research suggests that poor oral vocabulary may contribute to poor comprehension skills (Clarke *et al.*, 2010); therefore, it is important that discussion and questioning form the basis of lessons devised to teach and assess comprehension. The 'Simple View of Reading' (Gough and Tunmer, 1986), explored in Chapter 2, captures the idea that reading comprehension is dependent upon oral language skill, and according to this conceptual framework comprehension is taken to mean the understanding of spoken and written language. As listeners, children have to build a representation of what the speaker is saying based on what they already know; this has to be assimilated into their existing schema if effective comprehension is to take place. This information has to be processed by the listener in order to develop a conceptual understanding. Consequently, *the listener's general knowledge and level of cognitive development will have a bearing on the comprehension of the message* (Rose, 2006, p88). Therefore, it follows that structured discussion and guided conversations using picture books will ultimately benefit a child in terms of developing comprehension skills. For, in order to read and understand a text, children have to be able to understand language and all the nuances associated with implicit meaning which is often hidden in language – spoken and written.

Language comprehension

So, what do we mean by language comprehension? Language comprehension is the ability to understand speech. However, there are many forms of speech, ranging from formal to informal and it can be highly contextualised or abstract in nature. The listener is required to not only extract explicit meaning but also to draw inferences based upon what has been said and he or she may be required to read between the lines. Consider how someone answers when asked how they are feeling: the answer may be along the lines of 'fine', but subtle differences may be conveyed through intonation, gestures, facial expressions and choice of words. The listener has to deduce the speaker's perspective based upon what they hear and, to a certain extent, see. Therefore, children need to develop an understanding of voices, perspectives and viewpoints. This translates into children understanding the intent of the author and the illustrator when engaged in the reading of picture books.

The use of picture books for developing inference

According to O'Neill, in her article on reading pictures, illustrations are crucial in developing meaning for *there is much to be read from a picture, much to be inferred and understood implicitly as well as what is obviously depicted* (O'Neill, 2011, p222). Looking at pictures as a means of developing comprehension skills may not sit comfortably with some teachers but the benefits of addressing this in the classroom are evident (Clarke *et al.*, 2010). Rachael Levy presents her findings around young children's perceptions of themselves as readers in the Oakfield Study. It is interesting to note that children in Reception believed reading to be mainly about decoding print and because most of the children in the study perceived themselves as being unable to decode print, they did not recognise themselves to be readers (Levy, 2011). Thus, the ability to 'read' pictures was not seen as a recognised skill in the art of reading. However, there are many researchers in the field of education who celebrate the role of picture books in developing children's reading skills (Arizpe and Styles, 2003; Evans, 2009; Lewis, 2001; O'Neill, 2011). The emphasis on the printed word in school may sometimes preclude the use of pictures from being used to develop comprehension skills, but as you can see from the evidence above, the explicit teaching of picture-reading skills is crucial in developing children as 'readers'.

Inference skills for reading

In a review conducted by the National Foundation for Educational Research (NFER), the ability to draw inferences was recognised as a factor in predetermining reading skills (Kispal, 2008). There are a number of different types of inference outlined by various researchers and theorists, although for our purposes we will examine coherence and elaborative inferencing (Bowyer-Crane and Snowling, 2005; DfES, 2006).

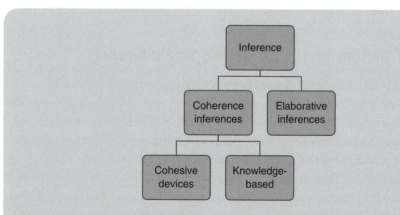

Figure 3.1 A representation of inference skills

Coherence inferences: these enable us to form a valid and reliable mental represen-tation of the text and can be classified in two ways as identified above (Figure 3.1). Cohesive devices enable us to make connections within the text. Consider the following example:

The cutlery was left in the drawer. It was still dirty.

To make sense of the sentences as a whole, we need to infer that 'it' in the second sentence was in fact the cutlery stated in the first sentence. Thus, cohesive devices (e.g. use of pronouns, etc.) enable us to construct a meaningful representation of what the author intended us to infer. Knowledge-based inferences rely on knowledge of the 'real world' in order to make sense of the text. They are often referred to as 'bridging inferences' as they bridge the gap between what is explicit within the text and what is implied. For example, the following sentences demand an understanding of context:

Alex was overcome by an uncontrollable thirst. He reached for the bottle of water.

We have to use our knowledge and experience of the world to infer that the water mentioned in the second sentence can be used to quench thirst as stated in the first sentence, and that Alex intends to drink this water. In effect, we have had to bridge the gap between what has been stated and what has been implied, thus generating the inference that Alex was making an attempt to satisfy his thirst. If we did not know this, the two sentences would not form a cohesive and comprehensive idea.

Elaborative inferences: these are generally knowledge based and embellish the text and may include inferences that are action based, predictive or speculative in nature. They rely widely on background knowledge and prior experience. For example:

The leopard, having escaped, leapt through the air. He landed perilously close to the ranger.

From these two sentences, it may be inferred that the leopard was somehow incarcerated because he is seen to 'escape'. We can also infer that the ranger may be injured; however, he may just as easily have avoided harm. These embellishments serve to enrich the nature of the text but are not vital to our understanding of the passage; we are still able to form a complete picture of what is happening.

In developing comprehension skills with young children, it is the latter type of inference that can be explored through picture books. Questions such as:

- What happens next?
- What do you think happens to the ranger?
- Where was the leopard?

will lead to a rich discussion in which children can infer what has happened.

Relevant background knowledge is an important factor in making inferences (Cain *et al.*, 2001; Pressley, 2000); therefore, it is imperative that we introduce children to new experiences and build on existing constructions so as to effectively extend background knowledge. Drawing upon a wide variety of texts and exposing children to different situations through role play will subsequently enable teachers to effectively teach inference by allowing children to question and develop their understanding of the world around them. By explicitly modelling the connections that we make, we are able to guide and support children in constructing meaning from texts using illustrations to make inferences based upon what we already know.

Teaching your class: Year 1

The lesson outlined below provides ideas for developing reading comprehension with your Year 1 class and suggests how you can help deepen understanding of character, mood and atmosphere as conveyed through illustrations. I have chosen to use Anthony Browne's *Hansel and Gretel* because the illustrations offer a rich source of information that will provoke discussion and allow children to make judgements based on what they can see in the text; it does not rely on the words in order for children to make sense of what is happening. Choose your own picture book based on the interests of your class or one that complements the current topic, but make sure the illustrations allow the story to unfold in a clear manner.

Context

The children in Year 1 have been listening to fairy stories and traditional tales, including 'Jack and the Beanstalk', 'Little Red Riding Hood', 'Goldilocks and the Three Bears' and 'The Three Little Pigs'. They have used Pie Corbett's *Bumper Book of Storytelling into Writing* (Corbett, 2006) to orally re-tell these stories based on the idea that learning to re-tell stories by heart, using actions, aids children's internalisation of language patterns and narrative structures; therefore, the children in Year 1 have a secure understanding of the structure of a fairy story/traditional tale. They have been encouraged to bring in favourite fairy stories from home and the role play area houses a variety of costumes to support the acting out of these stories. These have been recorded on tablets in order to assess children's understanding of narrative structure and understanding of this particular genre, including use of language features associated with fairy stories. To extend children's knowledge of key texts and to ensure that children are beginning to develop the skill *of making inferences on the basis of what is being said and done* (DfE, 2013, p21), the children are being introduced to alternative tales which do not follow the traditional and expected story line, for example:

- *Trust Me, Jack's Beanstalk Stinks! The Story of Jack and the Beanstalk as Told by the Giant* by Eric Braun;

- *The True Story of the Three Little Pigs* by Jon Scieszka;

- *The Three Horrid Little Pigs* by Liz Pichon;

- *Little Red* by Lynn Roberts.

All of the above have a rather delicious twist to the story, based on characters' viewpoints which have been explored through drama activities such as role play, hot seating and conscience alley.

Learning objectives

- To empathise with the main characters.

- To make inferences based on what is happening in the story.

- To participate in discussions about books.

Commentary

Even at a young age, children need to understand what *they are learning and* why. *It is not enough that the learning objective should be displayed; children in Year 1 need to have it explained so that they are absolutely certain of what it is they are learning and have the confidence to embark upon the task with a clear purpose. Through the use of success criteria, children will understand how they can be successful and can determine what excellence looks like with regard to the learning activity. This is explored in Shirley Clarke's book,* Active Learning Through Formative Assessment, *where she states that,* success criteria are the ingredients of the learning objective … the tools to be able to self- and peer-assess *(Clarke, 2008, p92).*

The learning objectives for this lesson are pivotal in laying the foundations for future work around reading comprehension. In this lesson, key skills around understanding authorial intent are developed and children are learning how participation in group discussion can extend and clarify ideas, leading to re-constructed understandings.

Introduction to the lesson

Provide groups of children with the book *Hansel and Gretel* by Anthony Browne and ask them to look carefully at the front cover, which depicts the two children sitting under a tree in the forest. Using sticky notes or recording devices, encourage children to formulate questions based on that picture. Each question must begin with 'I wonder why … ?' For example:

- I wonder why the children look so sad?

- I wonder who lives in the house behind the trees?

- I wonder where their mum is?

- I wonder why she has dirty knees?

Encourage all responses and provide prompts for those children who may find it difficult to ask questions.

Commentary

Early language experiences are important in developing comprehension skills (Bishop and Snowling, 2004; Catts et al., 2012), therefore providing time for children to talk to and listen to each other will contribute towards building vocabulary which will in turn aid comprehension. If a child has not met a word and used it in their spoken language, they are unlikely to be able to use it effectively in discussions. Activities such as 'I wonder ... ?' will not only allow children to share ideas, but will also contribute to wider vocabulary knowledge which may ultimately lead to an improved reading vocabulary (National Reading Panel, 2000).

During this activity, encourage and extend children's thoughts, eliciting responses that warrant further investigation. It is through your questioning that children will begin to develop and refine their ideas. Model good questioning techniques and verbalise your own thought processes when it comes to explaining your ideas about the picture on the front cover. How does it make you feel? Can you see anything unusual in the picture? What would you like to say to either of the children? Why? In this way, children are participating in a high level discussion and you, as the teacher, are able to assess understanding before embarking upon the main part of the lesson. This will enable you to group children accordingly in order to scaffold support effectively when they embark upon independent work.

Main lesson

Introduction

Explain to the children that they are going to put themselves in the shoes of the two main characters, Hansel and Gretel, in order to understand how they felt during certain parts of the story. Begin by reading the story to the children, asking them to predict what might happen next. Use talk partners to ensure that all children are engaged in the learning and listen in to their conversations in order to address any misconceptions around the narrative. Invite responses from individuals and add your own thoughts as to what might happen based on what has gone before.

Organise children into groups based on your assessment for learning during the introduction. Take your group of children outside to the 'forest school' area or to an area of the playground shaded by trees. If this is not possible, utilise the classroom to the best possible effect by clearing away some of the tables and chairs and maybe using an indoor tent to emulate the darkness of the forest. Images from the book can be placed around the area in order to initiate a trail. You may want to take one group of children to each picture in turn or divide the class into four or five groups and send each group to a different picture. Organisation and adult support will depend upon your individual setting and you will need to adjust accordingly.

The purpose of this lesson is for children to describe how the characters are feeling based upon what they have inferred from the pictures. Lead your group to each picture in turn and ask questions based on the illustration, asking children to notice the detail in the picture and encouraging them to suggest how Hansel and Gretel may be feeling. Follow up each question with: *how do you know?* or *what makes you think that?*, which will encourage children to explain and justify their replies. If you are unable to have a facilitating adult with each group, make use of apps which let you record questions that can be activated when a sound button is pushed (for example, book creator or skitch). Using tablets, try photographing an image from the book and adding recorded questions; children can then respond by recording their answers, allowing you to assess understanding following the lesson.

Commentary

Mixed-ability groups may be more appropriate in order to encourage a level of challenge and to allow those children who may have limited oral language skills to benefit from listening to and responding to a wider vocabulary. For those children who find it uncomfortable to articulate their views, being part of a group with confident speakers may encourage them to contribute; however, it is your job to ensure that you support and direct the discussion in order to elicit responses from all children.

Using questions to elicit responses and encourage higher order thinking skills is central to the learning taking place. Try to avoid closed questions that have a right or wrong answer; encourage children to think more deeply, using the pictures to inform their opinions about what is happening and how the characters are feeling. According to David Lewis (2001), children are part of a multimodal world where pictures, text and sound are combined; therefore, we should teach children to not only decode text but to also read the illustrations (Lewis, 2001). In order to do this effectively, we have to ask the 'right' questions. Use Bloom's taxonomy to focus your questioning to provide an adequate level of challenge for your learners. Bloom's taxonomy is usually represented as a pyramid; a hierarchy of thinking skills (Figure 3.2). There are different forms of the taxonomy available, since over time it has been redefined so as to more effectively reflect the learning that takes place in the classroom.

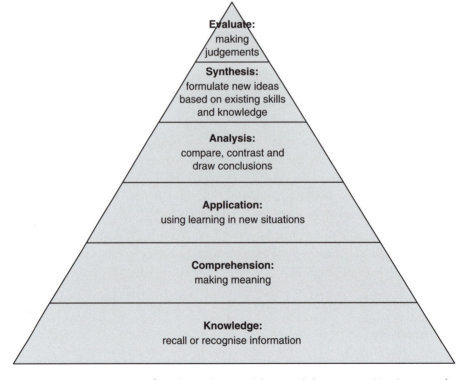

Figure 3.2 Bloom's taxonomy (based on a theoretical framework first presented in Bloom, 1956)

Below, you will find some useful questions (Figure 3.3) based on developing higher order questioning skills that can be used to extend children's observations and promote further discussion.

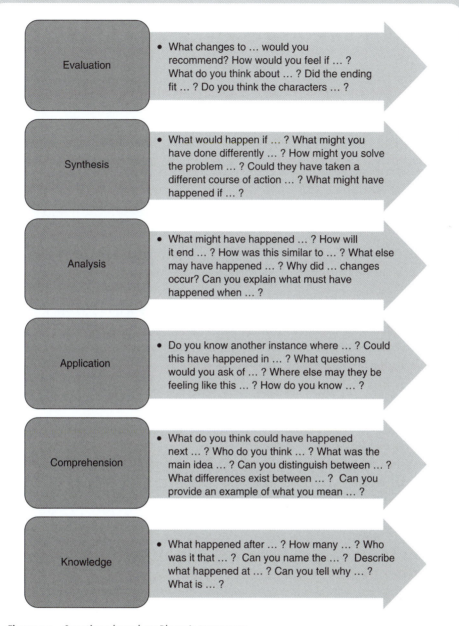

Evaluation

- What changes to … would you recommend? How would you feel if … ? What do you think about … ? Did the ending fit … ? Do you think the characters … ?

Synthesis

- What would happen if … ? What might you have done differently … ? How might you solve the problem … ? Could they have taken a different course of action … ? What might have happened if … ?

Analysis

- What might have happened … ? How will it end … ? How was this similar to … ? What else may have happened … ? Why did … changes occur? Can you explain what must have happened when … ?

Application

- Do you know another instance where … ? Could this have happened in … ? What questions would you ask of … ? Where else may they be feeling like this … ? How do you know … ?

Comprehension

- What do you think could have happened next … ? Who do you think … ? What was the main idea … ? Can you distinguish between … ? What differences exist between … ? Can you provide an example of what you mean … ?

Knowledge

- What happened after … ? How many … ? Who was it that … ? Can you name the … ? Describe what happened at … ? Can you tell why … ? What is … ?

Figure 3.3 Questions based on Bloom's taxonomy

Plenary

Divide the class into groups of four: one child takes on the role of Hansel, one takes on the role of Gretel and the other two children are going to ask some questions. The first pair needs to freeze frame a scene from the book so that the questioners can ask three questions of each character (Figure 3.4).

Figure 3.4 Visual card prompts

The visual nature of the cards will ensure that most children are confident to ask the questions. A teaching assistant or facilitating adult may also help children ask questions and articulate their answers. It is surprising how our youngest children are able to take on roles and suggest feelings, thoughts and words.

Pairs can then swap roles so that each has a turn at questioning and responding. During the plenary, listen in to their responses so that you can accurately assess their learning against the objectives. Encourage every child to self-assess by asking if they feel they know more about the characters Hansel and Gretel following their discussions with each other. Identify excellent responses and share these with the class so as to effectively clarify success. You may also want to scribe some of the responses to add to your working wall to build upon character analysis.

Commentary

Use the information gained around children's learning to inform subsequent lessons; listening in to these conversations will enable you to gain further insight into how well they have understood the lesson. There may be groups of learners for whom other opportunities to take part in guided discussions would be appropriate so as to further support the development of comprehension skills.

Assessment (measuring achievement)

Assessment for learning

- The introduction provides an excellent opportunity to assess the children in your class against the learning objectives, which will ensure you are providing appropriate support. Scaffolding and challenge for each learner will result in a personalised learning approach. Some children may have had extensive exposure to picture books and be very familiar with discussing characters; some children may have limited vocabulary which would benefit from a different type of questioning, building upon prior knowledge in a more systematic way, and some may require more explicit modelling in order to be able to contribute to a discussion.

- During the main teaching activity, you will continue to assess children based upon their responses to your questions and you can adapt your lesson to suit the needs of the learner. Remember to encourage children to articulate how they have reached their conclusions in order to develop a deeper level of understanding: if the children in your class are readily answering questions, you may need to develop their inference and deduction skills through the use of more sophisticated questions, using Bloom's taxonomy.

Assessment at the point of learning

- Ensure that anyone supporting children is fully aware of the purpose of the lesson so that they can make careful observations around the learning. Can children describe how the character is feeling? Can they justify why they think that? Use ongoing assessment to formulate more challenging questions based on Bloom's taxonomy to encourage a deeper understanding around characterisation, mood and atmosphere. Use questions to assess implicit understanding of what is inferred through the illustrations.

Assessment of learning

- Following your lesson, you will have the opportunity to reflect upon the learning that has taken place by reflecting upon written observations or recorded responses. Are there any surprises? Why might this be? Have you made any assumptions? Use the information gained to make assessments against the key criteria for this particular year group. Assessment frameworks will vary from school to school but should allow you to record progress and identify next steps. These can be communicated to children at the beginning of or during the next lesson.

- Because assessment will be based on children's verbal responses, you will need to pay particular attention to your questioning. Have you framed your questions in such a way as to ensure understanding? Have you provided each child with sufficient opportunity to meet the learning objectives? If not, additional teaching and learning opportunities will need to be built into subsequent planning to ensure a comprehensive assessment of each child can be made.

Challenges

- Some children may have limited language skills or a reduced oral vocabulary. It has been widely recognised that increased vocabulary leads to improved reading comprehension and developing readers are able to integrate newly learnt vocabulary into their existing language structure (Clarke *et al.*, 2010; Gough and Tunmer, 1986; Nation, 2005; National Reading Panel, 2000). Therefore, opportunities to extend vocabulary need to be included across the curriculum, which encourage children to discuss ideas and require specific modelling from the teacher in many cases.

- *The acquisition of two languages, with English as the additional language, must be a valuable attribute and should certainly not be seen as an obstacle to learning to read* (Rose, 2006, p23). Bilingual learners and those for whom English is an additional language have a range of experiences and understanding that they bring to the classroom. They may well be able to read texts in their first language and they will almost certainly have a varied vocabulary and oral language skills in their first language. Experiential learning and opportunities to practise and use social language are an integral part of extending their English vocabulary, and offer meaningful situations in which to practise and refine their language. The use of role play areas, barrier games and guided discussions all provide valid opportunities for development. When bilingual children engage in collaborative discussions and exploratory talk, they are able to build upon the language constructions of their peers in order to make meaning and develop not only their social language but also their cognitive language. Activities with a high contextual value, where language has a real purpose, are most successful in developing a wider vocabulary.

- Take care not to impose a ceiling on children's learning. From a very early age, children are able to construct meaning from pictures. Illustrations in picture books are a valuable method for developing meaning, and through structured conversations including questions such as: *how do you know that ... ?* and *tell me why you think that ...* children will begin to extend their reasoning skills. Do not simply ask the literal questions but challenge their thinking: make this a feature of your classroom.

Application of learning

Links to other areas of the curriculum

Language comprehension underpins all areas of the curriculum and, as teachers, we should explore every opportunity to engage children in informed and creative discussions, whether this is during a science experiment or when analysing a particular piece of music. Allowing children the time and space to air their views and offer personal insights is paramount in developing skills associated with comprehension. The lesson outlined above is relevant for developing these skills when teaching Year 1, although it is equally relevant if we were to be looking at a similar lesson for Year 6 children. How you develop thinking, through your choice of questions, will dictate the level at which you are building upon existing skills. Be familiar with the question stems outlined in Figure 3.3 so that every lesson becomes a lesson that can extend children's language comprehension.

Next lesson

Following on from the lesson outlined above, provide children with the opportunity to engage in small world play in order to extend and deepen their understanding of characterisation. Provide puppets or dolls so that children can act out their own interpretation of *Hansel and Gretel*. Ensure the role play area contains appropriate costumes so that your Year 1 class can act in role as the characters, thus providing opportunities for extending language and developing narrative understanding.

Learning outcomes review

You should now have an understanding of how language comprehension and reading comprehension are vital for extracting meaning from texts. The concept of text is taken to mean not only the written form but also visual and multimodal texts. You should also have ideas for extending children's answers through your questioning and how to structure conversations so that all children within the group feel confident to offer their own perspectives on a text. In addition, you should feel more confident when assessing children's understanding and identifying next steps in order to maximise learning potential for individuals.

The lesson plan outlined above illustrates one way in which you can achieve the learning objectives as set out for Year 1 children. It provides a structure that may be applied when teaching other texts or when facilitating guided reading sessions. It may be easily adapted to accommodate the needs of your class and may form part of a sequence of lessons or used as a standalone activity in order to explore characterisation in a meaningful and purposeful manner.

Further reading

Department for Education and Skills (DfES) (2006) Unit 2 Creating the learning culture: making it work in the classroom, in *Excellence and Enjoyment: Learning and Teaching for Bilingual Children in the Primary Years*. London: DfES.

This is a useful toolkit when considering best practice for teaching bilingual children in the primary classroom. It outlines ways in which children with English as an additional language can be supported to access curriculum content while also developing cognitive and academic language proficiency.

References

Arizpe, E and Styles, M (2003) *Children Reading Pictures: Interpreting Visual Texts*. London: Routledge Falmer.

Bishop, D and Snowling, M (2004) Developmental dyslexia and specific language impairment: same or different? *Psychological Bulletin*, 130: 858–86.

Bloom, BS (1956) *Taxonomy of Educational Objectives: The Classification of Educational Goals, by a Committee of College and University Examiners. Handbook I: Cognitive Domain*. New York: Longmans, Green.

Bowyer-Crane, C and Snowling, MJ (2005) Assessing children's inference generation: what do tests of reading comprehension measure? *British Journal of Educational Psychology*, 75 (2): 189–201.

Braun, E (2012) *Trust Me, Jack's Beanstalk Stinks! The Story of Jack and the Beanstalk as Told by the Giant.* Oxford: Raintree.

Browne, A (1981) *Hansel and Gretel.* London: Walker Books.

Cain, K, Oakhill, J, Barnes, MA and Bryant, PE (2001) Comprehension skill, inference-making ability, and their relation to knowledge. *Memory & Cognition*, 29 (6): 850–9.

Catts, H, Kamhi, A and Adolf, S (2012) Defining and classifying reading disabilities, in Kamhi, A and Catts, HW (eds.) *Language and Reading Disabilities* (3rd edn.). Boston, MA: Allyn & Bacon, pp45–76.

Clarke, PJ, Snowling, MJ, Truelove, E and Hulme, C (2010) Ameliorating children's reading comprehension difficulties: a randomized control trial. *Psychological Science*, 20: 1–11.

Clarke, S (2008) *Active Learning Through Formative Assessment.* London: Hodder Education.

Corbett, P (2006) *The Bumper Book of Storytelling into Writing Key Stage 1*. Wiltshire: Clown Publishing.

Department for Education (DfE) (2013) *The National Curriculum in England: Framework Document*. London: DfE.

Department for Education and Skills (DfES) (2006) *Developing Reading Comprehension (Primary Framework for Literacy and Mathematics)* [online]. London: DfES. Available at: **www.standards.dfes.gov.uk/ primaryframeworks/downloads/PDF/reading_comprehension.pdf**

Evans, J (ed.) (2009) *Talking Beyond the Page: Reading and Responding to Picturebooks*. London: Routledge.

Gough, PB and Tumner, WE (1986) Decoding, reading and reading disability. *Remedial and Special Education*, 7: 6–10.

Kispal, A (2008) *Effective Teaching of Inference Skills for Reading Literature Review: National Foundation for Educational Research*. London: DCSF.

Levy, R (2011) *Young Children Reading at Home and at School.* London: Sage.

Lewis, D (2001) *Reading Contemporary Picture Books: Picturing Text*. London/New York: Routledge Falmer.

Nation, K (2005) Reading comprehension difficulties, in Snowling, MJ and Hulme, C (eds.) *The Science of Reading*. Oxford: Blackwell, pp248–65.

National Reading Panel (2000) *Teaching Children to Read: An Evidence-Based Assessment of the Scientific Literature on Reading and Its Implications for Reading Instruction*. Washington DC: National Institute of Child Health and Human Development.

O'Neill, K (2011) Reading pictures: developing visual literacy for greater comprehension. *The Reading Teacher*, 65 (3): 214–23.

Pichon, L (2010) *The Three Horrid Little Pigs*. London: Tiger Tales.

Pressley, M (2000) What should comprehension instruction be the instruction of? in Kamil, ML, Mosenthal, PB, Pearson, PD and Barr, R (eds.) *Handbook of Reading Research: Volume III*. New York: Lawrence Erlbaum.

Roberts, L (2007) *Little Red.* London: Pavillion Children's Books.

Rose, J (2006) *Independent Review of the Teaching of Early Reading: Final Report*. London: DfES.

Scieszka, J (1989) *The True Story of the Three Little Pigs*. London: Puffin Books.

Chapter 4

Year 2: Developing reading comprehension through poetry

Learning outcomes

Poetry can all too often be perceived as problematic and is sometimes used solely as a way of exploring structure and identifying language features. This chapter addresses the teaching of comprehension skills through the use of poetry, building upon children's dialogue to explore meanings and suggesting ways in which you can develop comprehension through close examination of words and phrases that may initially lie beyond children's understanding.

This chapter will allow you to achieve the following outcomes:

- know how to structure and scaffold discussion to extend children's comprehension;
- understand how poetry can be used to explore authorial intent with children;
- develop teaching strategies that will facilitate and aid reading comprehension.

Teachers' Standards

Working through this chapter will help you meet the following standards:

3. Demonstrate good subject and curriculum knowledge.
4. Plan and teach well-structured lessons.
5. Adapt teaching to respond to the strengths and needs of all pupils.

Links to the National Curriculum

Year 2 programme of study

READING – Comprehension
Pupils should be taught to:

- develop pleasure in reading, motivation to read, vocabulary and understanding by:

  ✓ listening to, discussing and expressing views about a wide range of contemporary and classic poetry, stories and non-fiction at a level beyond that at which they can read independently
  ✓ discussing and clarifying the meanings of words, linking new meanings to known vocabulary
  ✓ discussing their favourite words and phrases
  ✓ continuing to build up a repertoire of poems learnt by heart, appreciating these and reciting some, with appropriate intonation to make the meaning clear

- participate in discussion about books, poems and other works that are read to them and those that they can read for themselves, taking turns and listening to what others say
- explain and discuss their understanding of books, poems and other material, both those that they listen to and those that they read for themselves.

(DfE, 2013)

Key focus: Encouraging dialogic and exploratory talk

Explicitly teaching comprehension skills increases children's ability to comprehend written texts (National Reading Panel, 2000; Pressley, 2006); therefore, effective modelling of strategies is necessary if children are to succeed in this area. The non-statutory guidance in the National Curriculum for English states that *thinking aloud when reading to pupils may help them to understand what skilled readers do* (DfE, 2013, p19), which builds upon the principles of guided reading as set out within the Primary National Strategy for English (DfEE, 1998), which encouraged teachers to articulate their thought processes when modelling reading.

Poetry offers a vehicle through which these strategies can be explored using children's responses and interpretations as a starting point. It also provides the perfect opportunity for teachers to think aloud in terms of their own responses and model how they have reached their conclusions. Through articulation of their thoughts, children should be able to clarify and refine their initial ideas around a poem and engage in purposeful discussion that explores themes, context and the writer's use of language. In order for this to work effectively in the classroom, we, as teachers, must ensure that poetry is not only explored and analysed, but celebrated for what it is: a genre to be enjoyed and experienced.

Activity

Consider the following questions carefully, noting your responses at the time:

- What was the last poem you read and how did it make you feel?
- When was the last time you heard a poem and how did you react?

Poetry is quite likely to evoke a personal response and this may be different for each individual. I can recall sharing 'The Lady of Shalott' by Alfred, Lord Tennyson (available at **www.bbc. co.uk/poetryseason/poems/the_lady_of_shalott.shtml**) with my Year 5 class and looking down to see two children with tears streaming down their cheeks. At that moment, I realised they had truly understood the significance of the final verse and I had connected with these two children through our reaction to the poem itself. Now, not every child exhibited such an intense reaction but, on some level, every child responded to the poem in a particular way.

The more that children are exposed to poetry, the greater the opportunities for expressing their personal opinions. This forms the basis of informed discussion. To do this, teachers need to be confident in what is available and appropriate within the world of poetry. A survey conducted with 1,200 primary teachers revealed that most had a very limited knowledge of children's poets, with 58 per cent of teachers in the survey only able to name one, two or even no poets (Cremin *et al.*, 2008). This echoed findings by OFSTED (2007), which reported that teachers in primary and secondary schools relied heavily upon a very narrow range of poets.

Activity

Try it for yourself:

Can you name six children's poets?

Of these, can you name at least two poems by each poet?

If you find this difficult, you may wish to refer to websites such as **http://childrenspoetryarchive. org/poets** and **www.booktrust.org.uk/books/children/poetry**, which have extensive lists and resources from which to draw.

Dialogic talk

To build upon children's responses to poems, we need to engage in the high level discussions that enable children to deepen their understanding and exercise their reasoning skills. Robin Alexander suggests that these conversations should be underpinned by the principles of dialogic teaching, which allow teachers and children to work together to listen, share ideas and co-construct meaning within a mutually supportive framework in order to reach a shared understanding (Alexander, 2008). Through engaging young children in conversations about poems, we can develop comprehension skills as we explore their reactions and responses to the poem and discuss the poet's perceived intent. This could take place during a guided reading session, as a whole class, on a one-to-one basis or as part of a book talk session as advocated by Aidan Chambers in his book *Tell Me: Children, Reading and Talk* (2011).

During a book talk session, the teacher guides the discussion through careful choice of questions, which enable children to question and rediscover understandings. He suggests that teachers

> *must ask the kinds of questions that help the readers discover and share their understanding of the bits that seem clear to them.*

> (Chambers, 2011, p138)

This can only be done through allowing and encouraging children to articulate their thoughts, however literal they may be. Building this dialogue within the group will ultimately lead to the purposeful talk that Alexander believes will encourage participants to answer questions in greater depth (Alexander, 2008).

Exploratory talk

As teachers, it is important that we know how children have interpreted the shared poems, therefore interaction between children and the teacher is the key to assessing understanding. There is no hiding from the fact that the role of talk is central to this and time has to be devoted to facilitating such discussions. Mercer and Littleton (2007) found that children who were more successful in comprehension tests were those who experienced classrooms where teachers guided understanding and were able to ask questions which led to reflection and reasoning in much the same way as suggested by Aidan Chambers within his 'Tell Me' framework (Chambers, 2011). In addition to this, children were encouraged to articulate their thought processes and collaborate with others to extend and reconstruct ideas around a text (Mercer and Littleton, 2007). A study of 500 classes across five countries conducted by Robin Alexander found that it was not uncommon in classrooms for teachers to ask questions which required limited response and did not always allow children to elaborate upon their first thoughts with children's exchanges often limited to five seconds or less (Alexander, 2008). This suggests that the teacher is in control of the discussion, and while this is necessary to some extent, Mercer suggests that it is the quality of the interactions as a group that can enrich the experience and deepen understanding: *consideration needs to be given to developing the talk repertoires of the pupils* (Mercer and Dawes, 2008, p10).

The following lesson plan offers practical ways in which this can be developed within your classroom; by facilitating discussion and dialogue that builds upon collaboration, comprehension skills can be greatly enhanced.

Teaching your class: Year 2

By Year 2, children should have experienced a number of different poems and will be developing an understanding of pattern and rhyme. Favourite picture books by Julia Donaldson including *The Gruffalo* and *The Snail and the Whale* together with other much loved favourites such as Michael Rosen's *We're Going on a Bear Hunt* will have undoubtedly made an appearance in Reception and Year 1. The following lesson develops children's understanding of poems through discussion and dialogue, building upon personal preferences and opinions and by using the poems 'What is Pink?' by Christina Rossetti (**www.poetryfoundation.org/poem/171954**) and 'The Moon' written by Robert Louis Stevenson (taken from an anthology collected by Roger Stevens, 2013, p46), the class will be introduced to poems that they may find difficult to access independently. In order to ensure the lesson is designed to meet the needs of your own Year 2 class, you may choose to use poems that are more suited to their interests or your current topic. However, remember to be guided by the need to expose children to a variety of classic poems which they can learn by heart and which they may be unable to read independently.

Context

The children in this Year 2 class are familiar with listening to poems and the class reading area contains a selection of poetry books from which they are able to choose and take home. Poems have been explored through guided reading sessions and they have had opportunities to demonstrate comprehension skills, particularly inference and deduction, through discussions with adults leading these sessions. The children are able to read the majority of these poems independently and are beginning to express preferences based upon what they are reading. They have been encouraged to read poetry for themselves through access to poems in anthologies included in the reading area; using audio clips to listen to favourite poems; and bringing in favourite poems from home. The class have listened to the two chosen poems so that they are becoming familiar with content and pattern.

Learning objectives

- To express personal views about a poem through discussion and dialogue.

- To understand the meaning of new vocabulary.

- To be able to understand and discuss a poet's choice of words and phrases.

Commentary

The objectives will be used to measure the learning that has taken place during the course of the lesson. Although one of the wider objectives will be for children to be able to recite by heart the poems, this will inevitably take place across a longer period of time. The objectives outlined above specifically relate to the pedagogical approach discussed earlier in this chapter: discussion and dialogue are integral features of developing reading comprehension and the ability to assimilate new vocabulary into existing frameworks will aid understanding of texts. Talk which supports purposeful discussion and dialogue will inevitably support comprehension; the processes by which children reach an understanding of the poems is pivotal to this lesson, therefore the skills identified above are of greater significance than the final product.

Introduction to the lesson

Choose a number of short poems to share with children as a whole class. Visual clips accessed from websites such as **www.bbc.co.uk/education** and **www.michaelrosen. co.uk** can also be used to add variety and allow children to experience poems read by others. Ask the children how the poem makes them feel. Children can respond using pre-prepared emoticon fans, as illustrated in Figure 4.1, to express their feelings about individual poems.

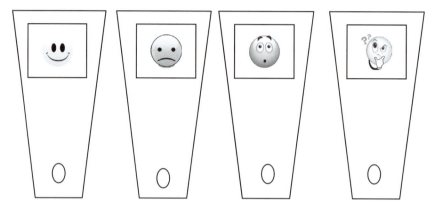

Figure 4.1 Emoticon fans

Encourage children to articulate their feelings using questions such as:

- Which part made you feel sad/happy/confused/surprised?

- Why do you feel … ?

- How did you decide?

- Tell me more about …

Use talk partners to ensure that all children are engaged in paired talk and have the opportunity to express their views, using adult support where necessary to elicit responses and explore answers in further detail.

Commentary

Comprehension involves a reader relating to the text; however, it is also about interpreting a text and evaluating it in terms of personal preference. As teachers you need to know how children have interpreted the text, in this case a poem, in order to assess understanding; therefore, interaction between teacher and child is vitally important (Browne, 2009). By allowing children to express their feelings towards a poem, they have the opportunity to demonstrate understanding. Using key questions to encourage children to explain how and why they have come to that decision will enable you to assess this understanding.

Through discussion of their responses to various poems, you are able to expose children to wider vocabulary, modelling and drawing upon good examples. Research has found that vocabulary development is a strong predictor of reading comprehension (Biemiller and Boote, 2006; Cunningham and Stanovich, 1997; Ricketts et al., 2007), therefore it follows that children should have opportunities to increase their vocabulary through discussion and exploration of words and phrases they have encountered when listening to unfamiliar poems.

Main lesson

Introduction

Depending upon adult support within the classroom, you may want to split the class into two so that one poem can be explored with each group. However you choose to organise the class, it is important that every child has the opportunity to talk about the poem with a teacher or a classmate during the course of this lesson.

Ask the children to listen to the poem read by you or pre-recorded in order to gain a 'feel' for the poem. Both 'The Moon' by Robert Louis Stevenson and 'What is Pink?' by Christina Rossetti work well for this activity, but you may have alternative classic poems that you prefer to share with your class. Refer to the starter activity and ask children to explain to a talk partner how the poem makes them feel. Allow the children to listen to the poem for a second time and ask them to return to their tables and draw the images that come into their minds. Both poems lend themselves well to visual representation and will enable you to assess children's literal understanding of the poem. Circulate during this activity, asking individual children for further clarification as to why they have included certain images.

Gather the children back to the carpet as a group and play or read the poem again. On this occasion read one line at a time and, using a variety of objects to represent each line, ask children to choose relevant objects to illustrate each line of the poem. For example, the following lines of the poem:

> *The moon has a face like the clock in the hall;*
> *She shines on thieves on the garden wall,*
> *On streets and fields and harbour quays,*
> *And birdies asleep in the forks of the trees.*
> *The squalling cat and the squeaking mouse,*
> *The howling dog by the door of the house,*

could be represented by a clock, a bag of gold coins, a number of toy boats, a small branch, a toy cat and a toy dog. Continue doing this for each line until you have a visual representation of the entire poem. This can be laid out on the floor or displayed on a table. If the poem is difficult to source in terms of objects, pin pictures to a washing line that runs across the classroom. The children will now have a visual reminder of the whole poem to which they can refer.

This lesson is focused upon opening up a dialogue for discussion and introducing children to new vocabulary, so it is important that words and phrases within the poem are explored. Provide a copy of the poem and five 10 pence coins between four children and explain that they have to choose five words and phrases that they particularly like or would like to explore further. However, each one of these words or phrases will cost them 10 pence, so they have to purchase wisely and there has to be a consensus of opinion. Allow time for them to read the poem together, ensuring that those children who may not be able to decode the words in the poem have adult support or are able to listen again to the poem on a recording device. These words and phrases can be highlighted or remembered in order to share with others during the course of the lesson. Use teaching assistants to scribe if appropriate for some groups of children.

You may wish to work with small groups of children to develop the discussion around their choice of favourite words and phrases or engage with the whole class. One way in which to organise this next part of the lesson may be to group children so that one member from each group joins with one from a different group until you have mixed groups of four. This will allow for a richer discussion as each individual will have to explain to the rest of the group their choice of words and phrases and, more importantly, justify this choice. While these discussions are taking place, prompt individuals with questions such as:

- What did you like about this phrase?

- How did it make you feel?

- Tell me what you think this word means?

- Where have you heard this word before?

- Why do you think the poet uses this word and not this word?

- Would you change any words? Why?

- Is there a word that you would like to know more about?

- Are there any words and phrases that you find difficult to understand?

- Do you think the words and phrases fit with the rest of the poem?

This will ensure that children think carefully about authorial intent in terms of word choice, and through discussing their favourite words and phrases with others they will have opportunities to argue, reason, justify and challenge.

Commentary

Engaging children with poetry is essential if you are to use it effectively to develop reading comprehension skills. In order to enhance understanding, poetry should be used, not purely as a model for writing, but as a means for creating purposeful dialogue. A report published by OFSTED (2007) stated that all too often, poetry was used as a framework for writing and that children were not given opportunities to reflect upon poems in a purposeful manner. The report went on to state that some of the best practice observed included teachers who routinely read poems with their classes for enjoyment and pleasure rather than to imitate writing styles. The result was that their pupils read a much wider range of poems and were able to talk more knowledgeably about them *(OFSTED, 2007). If your class are familiar with hearing poems read to them, they are more likely to engage in*

(Continued)

(Continued)

discussion in a critical manner, as they will not have the expectation that they will have to produce a written piece of work. Listening to poems will also extend their repertoire and if read well, will enhance the experience, leading to increased enjoyment and a desire to engage in discussions about that which they have enjoyed (Waugh and Jolliffe, 2013). If you are anxious about reading aloud in terms of expression and intonation, record the poem or use pre-recorded audio and visual clips from the internet which may enhance the experience for your class.

By repeating the poem, you are familiarising children with the poem and laying the groundwork for learning poems by heart as stipulated in the National Curriculum. Little and often seems to be the best way of learning by heart and through the use of visual prompts such as objects and pictures, you are aiding children's internalisation of the poem. Further strategies for encouraging children to learn poems by heart can be found in Off by Heart: Poems for Children to Learn and Remember *(Stevens, 2013).*

Discussion of favourite words and phrases is a requirement of the National Curriculum. By using an activity such as spending 50 pence to buy certain words and phrases, children have to think carefully about the choices they make in a fun and engaging manner. The purpose of this activity is to promote talk and encourage children to engage critically in conversation. This does not always happen automatically when we direct children to discuss a topic (Mercer and Dawes, 2008), therefore this may need to be modelled. Neil Mercer identified three types of talk that featured in classrooms:

(i) *Disputational talk – where participants often disagree and may only consider their own viewpoint.*
(ii) *Cumulative talk – non-critical and non-evaluative where most participants agree.*
(iii) *Exploratory talk – there is a shared purpose whereby participants are able to engage in a critical but constructive way in order to reach a shared agreement.*

(Mercer, 2000)

The children in classes where teachers used discussion and dialogue in order to promote exploratory talk within their classrooms achieved better results on reading comprehension tests. Effective teachers were able to guide understanding through their questioning; encouraged reflection and reasoning; allowed children to articulate their thought processes and encouraged the group to listen to other perspectives in order to re-construct their own opinions (Mercer and Littleton, 2007). This suggests that by providing children with the opportunity to discuss poems in this way and using key questions as identified above, your children in Year 2 will be more confident in their understanding of texts.

We found that raising awareness of the importance of exploratory talk, and teaching pupils exactly how to make it happen, does increase the incidence of exploratory talk, helping both primary and secondary children to learn successfully through discussion-based activities.

(Mercer and Dawes, 2008, p12)

Plenary

Employ hot seating during the plenary as a means to assess individual understanding. In pairs, one child becomes the interviewer, the other acts in role as the poet. The interviewer asks the poet why he or she chose to write a particular phrase and the other child has to answer in role, as though being interviewed for a TV programme or for a magazine article. These exchanges could be recorded so that answers may be analysed or used for assessment purposes. Refer to the learning objectives for this particular lesson and listen carefully to children's responses in order to inform next steps.

Commentary

By justifying their choice of particular words and phrases from our poem, 'The Moon' by Robert Louis Stevenson, children will be expressing their personal preference as to why they like a particular part of the poem. As the teacher, you will be able to assess understanding of unfamiliar vocabulary such as squalling, quays *and* howling *and the context in which it was used. Consider how this can be used to further extend vocabulary.*

Assessment (measuring achievement)

Assessment for learning

- The children need to be familiar with listening to poems and have experience of talking about them in small groups. Some children may find it difficult to articulate their views about a text; therefore, you may need to consider appropriate groupings.

- During the main body of the lesson, use answers to your key questions to inform your assessment for learning and provide an appropriate level of challenge based on their comments. Remember that challenge is appropriate for all children regardless of ability and if they do not have to think carefully before justifying an opinion, it may be because they are not receiving adequate challenge within the lesson.

Assessment at the point of learning

- Use sticky notes to record children's responses to some of your questions. Do they have an understanding of the meanings of various words and phrases? Can they use them in a different context? Why do they think the poet chose particular words? How does it improve the overall mood of the poem? If children are answering these questions, they are demonstrating good levels of comprehension by interpreting the poems and identifying the writer's viewpoint.

- It may be appropriate to work with a particular group in order to assess understanding or to tailor your questions more precisely to elicit a deeper understanding of the poem. If so, ensure that you are prepared with key questions that will inform assessment around purpose and the poet's viewpoint.

Assessment of learning

- Use your school's assessment framework to make summative assessments of children following this lesson. The information that you have both written and recorded can be used to support your judgement and provide evidence to demonstrate reading comprehension skills. You do not want to hoard unmanageable quantities of transcripts or endless sticky notes, therefore you will need to make a judgement based upon the criteria outlined in your school's assessment policy. Some evidence may be useful in supporting this.

- Remember that this lesson comprises one lesson within a series of lessons which may all contribute to forming an overall picture of where an individual child may lie in terms of assessment. Be alert to incidental evidence that may be demonstrated across the curriculum which supports children's ability to comment upon writers' viewpoints.

Challenges

- At the heart of reading comprehension lies the ability to make sense of a text and how the reader is able to interpret and evaluate that text. We have previously considered the role of oral vocabulary in this, but knowledge that a reader (oral listener) brings to a text is also of importance in comprehension because this knowledge is constructed within a social and cultural context (Mercer, 2000). Therefore, the meaning constructed from poems is dependent upon prior knowledge. This may explain why sometimes, children's responses to a text may seem irrelevant or unrelated. Questioning children's responses at this stage is one way in which you can gain an understanding of why a child may perceive the text in a particular way and will allow you to explore misconceptions. In the poem used for the lesson outlined above, if children are not familiar with *harbours* and *quays*, they are unlikely to be able to make sense of the significance of the line within the poem. This has implications for exploring prior knowledge. In a similar way, if a child is unfamiliar with a bat's sleeping habits, the idea that it resides in a bed may be taken literally! How do you find out what knowledge children have? The meaning derived from our poem may be different for individual children depending upon their prior knowledge, which may be in many ways based upon life experiences (Tennent, 2015).

Application of learning

Links to other areas of the curriculum

Children frequently encounter subject knowledge that may be unfamiliar when exploring history, geography or science topics. They will have to read and listen to texts that may require them to employ comprehension skills. The place of discussion and dialogue as outlined in this chapter is an important tool in constructing meaning; therefore, the types of questions that we use when discussing a story or a poem may aid understanding in other areas of the curriculum. Be confident in the questions that you need to ask in order to evaluate understanding.

Next lesson

Continue to encourage your class to learn the poem by heart through recitation and by using the objects chosen to act as a visual aide memoire. Maybe use actions when performing the poem based on Pie Corbett's storytelling technique in order to encourage internalisation of poetic structure (Corbett, 2006). Develop understanding of the poem by extending the role play opportunities started in the plenary. Hot seating of the poet will enable children to explain the meanings that they have gained from the poem. Contrast two poems by the same author, looking for similarities, differences and patterns. Are there any words and phrases that are repeated or used frequently? How does this enhance or detract from the meaning of the poem?

Learning outcomes review

You should now have considered how poetry can be used to support reading comprehension and have explored how this may be achieved within the classroom. You will also be aware of the statutory requirements for teaching poetry to Year 2 and have an understanding of what this may look like in terms of content and assessment. Discussion is an integral part of a reading comprehension lesson and needs to be planned in order to be successful. This chapter has demonstrated how the use of exploratory talk allows children the opportunity to reflect upon and justify their own personal preferences.

The suggested lesson can be adapted to suit the needs of your class and year group, for the principles of high-quality discussion remain the same regardless of age or phase. Carefully consider your choice of poems to use in the classroom so as to maximise learning potential. This will ensure that the strategies outlined above can be employed purposefully to develop children's full potential.

Further reading

Chambers, A (2011) *Tell Me: Children, Reading and Talk.* Stroud: Thimble Press.

This book explores how we can share texts with children and develop book talk in the classroom. Lots of practical ideas that can enhance the reading classroom.

Cremin, T, Mottram, M, Collins, F and Powell, S (2008) *Building Communities of Readers.* London: PNS/UKLA. Available at: **www.ukla.org/downloads/teachers_as_readers.pdf**

An interesting study around teachers' knowledge of texts and the benefits of teachers as readers in the classroom.

Mercer, N (2000) *Words and Minds: How We Use Language to Think Together.* London: Routledge.

This gives a comprehensive overview of the place of exploratory talk in the classroom.

www.poetryarchive.org and **http://childrenspoetryarchive.org**

This website features recordings of many poems so that poetry may be listened to and not just read.

References

Alexander, RJ (2008) *Towards Dialogic Teaching: Rethinking Classroom Talk* (4th edn.). York: Dialogos.

Biemiller, A and Boote, C (2006) An effective method for building meaning vocabulary in primary grades. *Journal of Educational Psychology*, 98 (1): 44–62.

Browne, A (2009) *Developing Language and Literacy 3–8*. London: Sage.

Chambers, A (2011) *Tell Me: Children, Reading and Talk*. Stroud: Thimble Press.

Corbett, P (2006) *The Bumper Book of Storytelling into Writing Key Stage 1*. Wiltshire: Clown Publishing.

Cremin, T, Mottram, M, Bearne, E and Goodwin, P (2008) Exploring teachers' knowledge of children's literature. *Cambridge Journal of Education*, 38 (4): 449–64.

Cunningham, AE and Stanovich, KE (1997) Early reading acquisition and its relation to reading experience and ability 10 years later. *Developmental Psychology*, 33 (6): 934–45.

Department for Education (DfE) (2013) *The National Curriculum in England: Framework Document*. London: DfE.

Department for Education and Employment (DfEE) (1998) *The National Literacy Strategy: Framework for Teaching*. London: DfEE.

Donaldson, J and Scheffler, A (1999) *The Gruffalo*. London: Macmillan Children's Books.

Donaldson, J and Scheffler, A (2003) *The Snail and the Whale*. London: Macmillan Children's Books.

Mercer, N (2000) *Words and Minds: How We Use Language to Think Together*. London: Routledge.

Mercer, N and Dawes, L (2008) The value of exploratory talk, in Mercer, N and Hodgkinson, S (eds.) *Exploring Talk in School*. London: Sage.

Mercer, N and Littleton, K (2007) *Dialogue and the Development of Children's Thinking: A Socio Cultural Approach*. London: Routledge.

National Reading Panel (2000) *Teaching Children to Read: An Evidence-Based Assessment of the Scientific Literature on Reading and Its Implications for Reading Instruction*. Washington DC: National Institute of Child Health and Human Development.

OFSTED (2007) *Poetry in Schools: A Survey of Practice 2006/7*. London: OFSTED.

Pressley, M (2006) *Reading Instruction that Works: The Case for Balanced Teaching*. New York: The Guilford Press.

Ricketts, J, Nation, K and Bishop, DV (2007) Vocabulary is important for some, but not all reading skills. *Scientific Studies of Reading*, 11 (3): 235–57.

Rosen, M (1989) *We're Going on a Bear Hunt*. London: Walker Books.

Stevens, R (2013) *Off by Heart: Poems for Children to Learn and Remember*. London: A&C Black.

Tennent, W (2015) *Understanding Reading Comprehension: Processes and Practices*. London: Sage.

Waugh, D and Jolliffe, W (2013) *English 5–11: A Guide for Teachers*. London: Routledge.

Chapter 5

Year 3: Oral storytelling and reading comprehension

Learning outcomes

Storytelling is a powerful tool in the classroom but one that you might not immediately relate to developing comprehension skills. Active engagement, collaboration and interaction between the storyteller and the listeners can greatly enhance children's ability to make sense of a story and gain a greater understanding of the subtle complexities that lie within a text.

This chapter will allow you to achieve the following outcomes:

- understand how storytelling can be used to develop comprehension skills;
- consider what constitutes effective storytelling;
- be able to reflect upon how this can be used in lessons to encourage dialogue, participation and collaboration.

Teachers' Standards

Working through this chapter will help you meet the following standards:

3. Demonstrate good subject and curriculum knowledge.
4. Plan and teach well-structured lessons.
5. Adapt teaching to respond to the strengths and needs of all pupils.
6. Make accurate and productive use of assessment.

Links to the National Curriculum

Year 3 programme of study

READING – Comprehension
Pupils should be taught to:

- develop positive attitudes to reading and understanding of what they read by:

- ✓ listening to and discussing a wide range of fiction, poetry, plays, non-fiction and reference books or textbooks
- ✓ increasing their familiarity with a wide range of books, including fairy stories, myths and legends, and retelling some of these orally
- ✓ identifying themes and conventions in a wide range of books
- ✓ discussing words and phrases that capture the reader's interest and imagination

- participate in discussion about both books that are read to them and those they can read for themselves, taking turns and listening to what others say.

(DfE, 2013)

Key focus: Using oral storytelling to develop comprehension

We are well versed in the benefits of reading stories to our children, but how often do we *tell* stories in our classrooms? Maybe you have taken your children outside to re-enact *We're Going on a Bear Hunt* (Rosen, 1989) or re-told the story of 'Goldilocks and the Three Bears' from memory, but have you ever told a story that you have made up on the spot? It is not easy to think on your feet when you have a class of 30 children looking up expectantly at you; however, after reading this chapter, you will come to appreciate the benefits of using this pedagogical approach within your classroom.

Storytelling opens up children's imaginations and allows them to enter another realm inside their minds. In order to make sense of the story, they have to listen carefully, make links between events, empathise with characters and appreciate the complexities of cause and effect. Storytelling encourages children to use their visual imagination and create pictures in their minds, since they do not have illustrations from which to draw clues (Isbell *et al.*, 2004). It also allows children to develop confidence, improve self-esteem and provides opportunities for children to make sense of the world around them. We have only to observe children in an Early Years classroom to understand how children interpret their own experiences through drama and role play.

Activity

Choose a familiar story book and practise telling the story aloud without relying on the words and pictures. How do you use your voice to signal changes in characters' feelings? Does your posture alter when speaking in role? Do you use your body to indicate tension, friction, joy? Can you remember the story? Have you changed any parts?

Tell this story to your class rather than reading it from the book and ask them if they enjoyed it. Ask questions to assess their understanding and compare it with the times when you may have read a story to them.

A number of studies conducted around storytelling have concluded that telling stories in the classroom can develop comprehension for reading (Craig *et al.*, 2001; Peck, 1989; Trostle and Hicks, 1998). Storytelling, when combined with effective questioning which allows children to reflect upon the story, can improve children's ability to answer questions on an inferential and critical level. Children are able to employ the same skills when listening to a story as they are when reading a story. One of the benefits of using storytelling to develop comprehension is its inclusive nature: children do not need to decode words to gain an understanding. They are able to experience the story through the storyteller's interpretation, taking account of his or her facial expressions, tone of voice and body language to infer meaning. In exactly the same way in which picture books can be used to encourage discussion and dialogue, oral stories can do the same. Oral stories have the added benefit of narrative structure; a story unfolds and events are linked across time and place. Stories encourage children to map this in their heads, look for answers and begin to use similar structures in their own writing.

When children engage in storytelling for themselves, as outlined in the lesson guidance below, they have opportunities to develop their comprehension skills through participation. They learn to build a sense of a story, ensuring there is a logical structure. They will also have opportunities to develop an understanding of authorial voice, which can be physically demonstrated through storytelling. As children increase their understanding of a sense of a story, they will become more proficient in predicting, summarising and evaluating a text, which all serve to contribute to the development of comprehension skills.

Activity

Challenge yourself by taking a famous painting, for example John William Waterhouse's *The Lady of Shalott* (1888) or *A Sunday Afternoon on the Island of La Grande Jatte* by Georges Seurat (1884) and create a story based on what you observe in the picture. Consider the skills you have employed in order to make sense of the painting and how your understanding of story structure and characterisation has informed your narrative. Now list the skills that the children in your class will need to possess in order to construct their own story: how will you model these in the classroom?

When you feel confident, share this with your class and encourage them to do a similar activity based around favourite pictures or paintings.

Teaching your class: Year 3

Oral storytelling can help build upon children's understanding of texts and allows them opportunities to demonstrate their awareness of narrative and characterisation: two important elements in developing comprehension skills. The following lesson draws upon and extends children's knowledge of myths and legends; an area of literature that is embedded in the National Curriculum for lower Key Stage 2 children. There are many myths and legends that can be used in the classroom, most of which have a predictable structure, generic themes and specific language features. Therefore, choice of stories will be down to personal preference and topic choices for individual classes. In the lesson exemplified below, I will concentrate on one or two key legends, but the way in which the lesson addresses children's learning can be applied to any story: it is the value of the oral storytelling in developing comprehension skills that will be at the heart of the lesson.

Context

As part of their English lessons, the children in Year 3 have been exploring Greek myths, including: 'Theseus and the Minotaur', 'Daedalus and Icarus' and 'Perseus and Medusa'. Using Pie Corbett's *Bumper Book of Storytelling into Writing* (Corbett, 2006) as a frame, they have had opportunities to orally re-tell these stories to children in Year 1, using actions to enhance their performance. Up until now, the lessons have been focused on developing a sense of narrative, allowing children to internalise story structure so that they are more proficient in writing their own myths. They have an understanding that myths have common features.

- Set in a distant land, for example a faraway island or a mountainous region.

- Takes place in the past.

- The plot is usually based around a journey, a quest or a series of trials.

- Includes a fantastical beast with supernatural powers.

- An interesting setting, for example an island, a mountain, a desert.

- There is a hero.

- The hero has to overcome obstacles in order to be successful in his quest.

In addition, children in Year 3 have watched video clips of storytellers (see further reading below) telling stories and made notes on effective storytelling techniques. These include:

- facial expressions;

- intonation;

- tone of voice;

- body language;

- camera angle;

- visual effects.

They will be using these techniques to engage their listeners and secure audience participation.

Learning objectives

- To identify and use effective storytelling techniques.

- To understand the key features of a myth.

- To employ comprehension strategies to demonstrate understanding of a story.

- To use language for a particular purpose and audience.

Commentary

The learning objectives each refer to a particular skill that needs to be developed over the course of the lesson. They are specific and measureable in terms of achievement for learners. The class have previously identified effective storytelling techniques, but during this lesson they will need to apply them to engage the listener. The lesson outlined below will provide children with opportunities to demonstrate their understanding of myths and during the modelled session, the teacher will need to assess individual learners' capacity to comprehend the text and make an informed judgement as to how well they employ strategies to make sense of the narrative.

The fourth learning objective is specifically drawn from the National Curriculum programmes of study and will allow children to demonstrate their understanding of purpose and audience; a fundamental skill when interrogating authorial intent in written texts.

Introduction to the lesson

Divide children into groups of three according to their reading ability and provide a copy of the same story for each member of the group, differentiated for each group. Each story is unfinished, with the ending missing. Ask children to read their story independently, paying particular attention to what is happening in the story and consider what might happen at the end. Explain that they are going to put the text away and take turns to re-tell part of the story. They must then decide who will go first, second and third and take turns to tell the story, stopping at a convenient point for the next member of the group to continue until they have re-told the story up until the point where the ending is missing. They must then share what they think will happen at the end of the story, based on their perceptions of the ongoing narrative. Listen in to these conversations and ask adult helpers in the classroom to make notes based on their observations. Alternatively, ask children to use tablets to record their stories so that you can access them following the lesson in order to assess understanding.

Commentary

This activity is designed to enable you, as the teacher, to assess their understanding of what they are reading. You will have matched the text to children's reading ability based on your assessment of their word recognition skills for it is their comprehension that is being assessed at this point. By re-telling the story in the correct sequence, the children have to engage with the text to construct meaning. The National Reading Panel suggest that readers derive meaning from text when they engage in intentional, problem solving thinking processes *(National Reading Panel, 2000, p14). By allowing children to construct their own conclusion to the narrative, this activity will draw upon their problem solving skills and require children to employ inference and deduction skills in order to construct a meaningful and appropriate end to the story.*

While the groups are engaged in the re-telling of their stories, assess their metacognitive awareness; have they used strategies that help them make sense of the text? Do they recognise when events do not seem to follow a logical pattern? How do they overcome these problems? This will help to provide a better picture of individuals' ability to comprehend a text based on what they know and their awareness of what they need to know. By making these links within the text, children will be demonstrating a number of key comprehension strategies.

Careful assessment of children's abilities during this introductory activity will enable you to group children effectively for the main part of the lesson.

Main lesson

Introduction

Ask children to list the key features of a myth on mini whiteboards or large pieces of paper. Use this information to clarify misconceptions or tease out any features that the class may have forgotten. Explain that the class is going to be working in groups of four to prepare their own story that they will tell to a group of younger children. They will need to demonstrate effective storytelling techniques to engage the reader and be able to elicit audience participation. However, instead of using familiar stories, they will need to formulate their own myth based on a picture that will be provided. This picture will include characters, setting and a number of objects and artefacts that will have to be used to construct an appropriate narrative.

Use clip art to prepare a story mat containing an image of a Greek hero, a mysterious island, an embellished sword, a jewelled necklace and a mythical beast. Model telling the story based on the picture displayed, employing effective storytelling techniques as outlined above. You will need to have prepared this part of the lesson so that your story flows and you are able to demonstrate the strategies that you wish the children to employ when they deliver their story to a Year 1 class.

While telling the story of the Greek hero's quest to find the jewelled necklace, encourage the children to build pictures in their head of the voyage to the mysterious island and the encounter with a hideous beast. Emphasise the interactive nature of storytelling, encouraging audience participation by asking questions to clarify understanding and inviting the audience to ask questions so that you can elaborate upon the events of the story. Try to include a repetitive element so that the audience can join in with the oral language. All the time, use a 'think aloud' approach whereby you verbalise your thought processes, explaining why you are employing various strategies. For example, when narrating the hero's first meeting with the mythical beast, demonstrate the power that the hero has by standing tall and speaking with a deep, authoritative tone. Tell your class that the reason you are doing this is to convey the impression that the hero is a strong and powerful figure who will be able to defeat his enemy. Ask the children why you are cowering when describing how the hero moves towards the beast, brandishing his magical sword. Do they understand how characteristics are conveyed through voice, body and gesture? By making this explicit, the children in your class will mirror these strategies and draw on these when delivering their own story to the Year 1 class, ensuring a successful storytelling session.

Explain that each group will receive a story mat or you could direct each group to access a myth generator such as the one found at **http://teacher.scholastic.com/ writewit/mff/mythmachine.htm** so that they have a hero, a mythical beast, a setting and an object upon which to base their story.

They must then work in small groups to construct a story containing all the features of a myth and using effective storytelling techniques to showcase later in the week. Allow children to video their storytelling using tablets or flip recorders so that they are able to improve and refine their techniques. This will also provide valuable opportunities for the group to discuss and adapt their story.

Commentary

This activity has a number of purposes in terms of improving, enhancing and demonstrating comprehension skills. It has been recognised by some researchers that storytelling is a powerful tool for teaching a sense of a story and for improving comprehension skills (Isbell et al., 2004; Peck, 1989; Strickland and Morrow, 1989). As the story unfolds, children begin to construct a mental representation of the action that is taking place. Because there are very few pictures upon which to base their thoughts, children will rely on their visual imagination to 'follow' the story. By allowing the children to participate in the storytelling, you are employing a pedagogical strategy that encourages interaction; through questions you are inviting opinions and building upon the social element of language. This will, in turn, enable children to comment on and articulate their own thoughts around the story, thus demonstrating effective comprehension (Miller and Pennycuff, 2008).

In order to successfully interact with the storyteller, the audience has to engage in active listening, developing an understanding of story structure by building upon what has gone before. During storytelling sessions, you will make greater eye contact with your listeners, thus increasing engagement. Your use of gestures, facial expressions and intonation all contribute to ensuring effective listening; whereas sometimes it is easy to 'drift away' when listening to a text being read or when reading to oneself, it is much more difficult to avoid listening to an animated storyteller. According to research conducted by Isbell et al. (2004), those children who heard stories told demonstrated greater comprehension in terms of exploring character, setting and themes.

By actively modelling the techniques that we want children to employ in their own storytelling, we can demonstrate the interaction between the storyteller and the listener, which is fundamental when we come to explore and comprehend texts. The storyteller conveys his or her interpretation of the story through use of body language, voice and gesture: an author will convey a story through use of language, grammatical features, themes and content. Providing children with the opportunity to participate in storytelling sessions will help to prepare them when commenting upon authorial tone and intent when reading.

Plenary

Organise the class so that two groups are sitting together. One group must outline their story in no more than five sentences; the other group must listen carefully and then formulate two questions based on what they have heard and record them on sticky notes or by means of a recording device (tablets, talking postcards or easispeak microphones). These may be asking for more information about an event or a character or questioning how the group will engage the audience. The other group then have the opportunity to do the same. Each group must identify an area for improvement based on peer feedback and record this in their books or on a sticky note so that you are able to reflect upon these following the lesson and use the targets to tailor your teaching during the next lesson.

Commentary

This will be an invaluable opportunity to assess children's comprehension skills. By listening to the questions that the groups ask, you will be able to assess their understanding of plot, character, themes and setting. Through monitoring the other group's five sentence summary of their story, you can assess comprehension of the genre and address any misconceptions immediately through your own careful questioning.

Assessment (measuring achievement)

Assessment for learning

- The introduction allows the teacher to make informed judgements of children's comprehension skills based upon their re-telling of a story. By predicting the ending, children will have to activate prior knowledge, construct mental images, summarise the main body of the text and analyse the text so as to ensure an appropriate and relevant ending; all key comprehension strategies (DfES, 2005). The information gleaned from this introductory activity will ensure that groups are appropriately organised to ensure support is directed in an effective manner. This may mean that one group is supported by a facilitating adult who can direct questions that will support and challenge thinking and scaffold learning. On the other hand, an element of further challenge could be incorporated into the main body of the lesson so as to ensure more able learners are sufficiently stretched in terms of their learning.

Assessment at the point of learning

This will take the form of observations. Key questions to ask yourself may include the following:

- Which children are demonstrating effective storytelling techniques?

- Are all children participating in the storytelling session?

- Are all children able to predict the ending based on prior knowledge?

- Can children justify their explanations based on prior knowledge?

- Can all children interpret the storyteller's intentions based on visual clues?

- Do the questions that children ask reflect their understanding of the narrative?

- Do the questions that children ask reflect their understanding of characters?

By addressing these key questions, you will be able to assess each child's progress against the learning objectives and address misconceptions or misunderstandings as they occur.

Assessment of learning

Following your lesson, it is important that you reflect upon the learning that has taken place. Have the children achieved the learning objectives set at the beginning of the lesson?

- Have children correctly employed storytelling techniques? How do you know? Does this demonstrate effective understanding of the story in terms of plot, narrative, character, themes and setting?

- Are they using appropriate models of narrative upon which to build their stories?

- Are children engaging with and responding to the narrative when actively involved either as a listener or as the storyteller?

- Do the questions from the plenary demonstrate understanding of the story? How do they relate to the events of the story?

Challenges

- An obvious challenge facing children when embarking upon storytelling is confidence. Some children may feel self-conscious relating stories to an audience, therefore it is necessary to provide opportunities for partner work whereby children can re-tell stories in pairs. Telling stories can develop social skills and collaborative practice, therefore careful organisation of pairs and groups will allow children to flourish in a secure and non-threatening environment. Encourage individuals to share a familiar story so that they do not necessarily have to consider the structure; allow them to sequence events and guide them towards implementing storytelling techniques such as making eye contact, adding gestures when appropriate so as to build confidence. By sharing stories with others, children will develop self-confidence as they discover that others are genuinely interested in listening to what they have to say.

- A storyteller does not have to be a 'performer' but requires a good memory and the ability to listen and react to subtle shifts in attention. They also need to know the story well and have the confidence to deliver it to an audience. This may seem a little daunting for some teachers, therefore if you would rather someone else modelled the storytelling, take a look at websites such as **www.bbc.co.uk/schoolradio/subjects/history/ancient_greek_myths**, which allows children to listen to myths being read aloud or access video clips of professional storytellers. Stopping the clip at pertinent moments to explore the storyteller's use of voice, intonation, gesture and content will facilitate discussions around effective practice. However, you may want to practise these techniques yourself in order to foster the relationship between yourself as a storyteller and your class as the listeners. Begin by re-telling a familiar story, adding voices for characters or use puppets or props to deflect attention from you as the speaker. Be flexible, avoid a script and be prepared to expect the unexpected when dealing with reactions from your audience. The hard work will be worthwhile as you take them on that magical journey through their mind's eye.

Application of learning

Links to other areas of the curriculum

Storytelling lends itself to all areas of the curriculum. As you develop these skills, use them to take children on a historical journey, allowing them to listen to factual events while creating pictures in their mind. Storytelling develops children's ability to connect prior knowledge and experience with the bigger picture; they will be able to link events in history or picture the journey of a river as you engage them in the storytelling. Storytelling does not have to be fictional.

By developing children's capacity to orally tell stories, you are increasing their confidence, their self-esteem and their ability to manipulate language. They will have an awareness of audience and purpose and *become more familiar with and confident in using language in a greater variety of situations, for a variety of audiences and purposes, including through drama, formal presentations and debate* (DfE, 2013, p24).

Next lesson

To a greater extent, your assessment will dictate the direction of your next lesson; however, you will need to consider how you build upon previous experiences and ensure progression in learning. Having spent time constructing and refining their stories, the children in your class will need time to rehearse and consolidate their performance. Just as we would expect children to re-draft and edit their writing, they will need time to edit their performance. This is a perfect opportunity to practise and challenge their comprehension of texts through careful questioning that promotes problem solving. Pose questions such as: why does the hero choose to do that? How do you think he feels? What would happen if he had chosen to embark upon a different journey? What would happen if the beast had defeated the hero? These questions allow children to talk through their thought processes and give reasons for their choices based on the narrative; it provides the *dialogic space for discussion* (Tennent, 2015, p161) which improves children's comprehension of texts.

Learning outcomes review

You should now have a greater understanding of the place of storytelling in the curriculum and how it can effectively enhance comprehension skills. Through the lesson plan and commentary, you should have an awareness of techniques and strategies that will help you teach effective storytelling and how this relates to the development of inference and deduction skills, characterisation and narrative structure. You should feel more confident in using these techniques within the classroom and in guiding children through reflective discussions about their stories. You should be able to facilitate informed discussion and dialogue, building on key developmental points. Interaction is crucial in ensuring that storytelling as a pedagogical strategy is successful and you will have had opportunities to reflect upon implementing this in your own classroom.

Further reading

There are a number of websites that offer tips and techniques that can support you in your storytelling endeavours:

http://dramaresource.com/strategies/story-telling

www.literacytrust.org.uk/assets/0000/0865/Storytelling_tips.pdf

www.sfs.org.uk/aboutsfs

The following websites focus on myths and legends and provide a plethora of stories and video clips to explore with your class:

http://myths.e2bn.org/teachers

www.bbc.co.uk/education/topics/zmvv4wx

References

Corbett, P (2006) *The Bumper Book of Storytelling into Writing Key Stage 1*. Wiltshire: Clown Publishing.

Craig, S, Hull, K, Haggart, A and Crowder, E (2001) Storytelling: addressing the literacy needs of diverse learners. *Teaching Exceptional Children*, 43 (5): 46–51.

Department for Education (DfE) (2013) *The National Curriculum in England: Framework Document*. London: DfE.

Department for Education and Skills (DfES) (2005) *Understanding Reading Comprehension: 1 What is Reading Comprehension?* Norwich: DfES.

Isbell, R, Sobol, J, Lindauer, L and Lawrence, A (2004) The effects of storytelling and story reading on the oral language complexity and story comprehension of young children. *Early Childhood Education Journal*, 32 (3): 157–63.

Miller, S and Pennycuff, L (2008) The power of story: using storytelling to improve literacy learning. *Journal of Cross-Disciplinary Perspectives in Education*, 1 (1): 36–43.

Morrow, LM (1985) Reading and retelling stories: strategies for emergent readers. *The Reading Teacher*, 38 (9): 870–5.

National Reading Panel (2000) *Teaching Children to Read: An Evidence-Based Assessment of the Scientific Literature on Reading and Its Implications for Reading Instruction*. Washington DC: National Institute of Child Health and Human Development.

Peck, J (1989) Using storytelling to promote language and literacy development. *The Reading Teacher*, 43 (2): 138–41.

Rosen, M (1989) *We're Going on a Bear Hunt*. London: Walker Books.

Strickland, DS and Morrow, LM (1989) Emerging readers and writers/oral language development: children as storytellers. *The Reading Teacher*, 43 (3): 260–1.

Tennent, W (2015) *Understanding Reading Comprehension: Processes and Practices*. London: Sage.

Trostle, SL and Hicks, SJ (1998) Effects of storytelling versus story reading on British primary children's comprehension and vocabulary acquisition. *Reading Improvement*, 35 (3): 127–36.

Chapter 6

Year 3: Reading non-fiction

Learning outcomes

Being able to make independent choices about what type of text will help us achieve a goal and being able to use a range of strategies to access texts efficiently is the sign of a purposeful reader. This chapter will look at the move from learning to read to reading to learn by enabling children to apply their understanding of how to access non-fiction for information.

This chapter will allow you to achieve the following outcomes:

- know the different roles of a successful reader;
- understand the implications of each role and how it can act as a barrier to or enabler of reading;
- develop an awareness of how non-fiction can inspire and motivate reading.

Teachers' Standards

Working through this chapter will help you meet the following standards:

1. Set high expectations which inspire, motivate and challenge pupils.
2. Promote good progress and outcomes by pupils.
3. Demonstrate good subject and curriculum knowledge.

Links to the National Curriculum

Years 3 and 4 programme of study

READING – Comprehension
Pupils should be taught to:

- develop positive attitudes to reading and understanding of what they read by:
    - ✓ listening to and discussing a wide range of fiction, poetry, plays, non-fiction and reference books or textbooks
    - ✓ reading books that are structured in different ways and reading for a range of purposes

- understand what they read, in books they can read independently, by:

  ✓ retrieve and record information from non-fiction.

(DfE, 2013)

Key focus: Utilising the roles of a successful reader

Activity

What is a successful reader? Label the picture below (Figure 6.1) with the key skills, knowledge and understanding you think a reader needs in order to be considered successful.

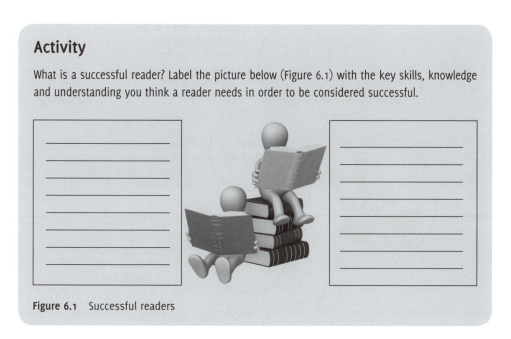

Figure 6.1 Successful readers

Issues of reading and reading success are tied up in debates over the nature of literacy and illiteracy. In order to be an active member of a literate society one must first understand the paradigms within which the society is operating: how do they conceptualise literacy? What are the accepted indicators of competency? In terms of reading, which is an activity that takes place largely within one's own head, it is difficult to provide evidence of individual success other than by outcome. In other words, you may or may not understand what you have just read, but until someone asks you a question about it there will be no external evidence either way and thus no way to check. And even once the question is posed, who gets to decide what the correct answer is?

In their journal article 'Literacies programs: debates and demands in cultural context', Freebody and Luke (1990) explored reading as a socioculturally and historically situated event. They identified four interrelated roles that constitute reading: Code-Breaker, Text Participant, Text User and Text Analyst (see Figure 6.2).

Janks (2014) re-designated Code-Breaker as Text Decoder when she used this model to help explain language and position in critical literacy (more on this, and on the role of Text Analyst, in Chapter 7), but recent debates about decoding in terms of phonemic awareness mean this has become a loaded term. Code-breaking does include understanding and using grapho-phonic cues, but it is also about understanding the grammatical structures particular to the language being used. In the current National Curriculum for England (DfE, 2013) much of the focus of early reading instruction is on teaching the role of the Code-Breaker.

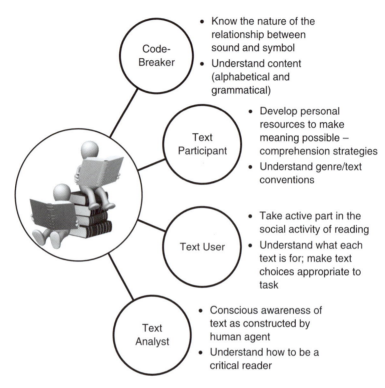

Figure 6.2 Diagram to summarise the four related roles of a successful reader (Freebody and Luke, 1990)

Activity

Think about the following sentence:

What called you?

In English this sentence sounds incorrect, although we understand what it is asking for; however, in other languages this would be the appropriate way of structuring the question.

- List three different ways English speakers could correctly rephrase the question to fit the grammatical 'code'.
- Punctuation is another set of symbols involved in a language's written code: identify three punctuation marks that are *not* used in written English.

Participating in reading non-fiction

Because the lesson described in this chapter is focused on the role of Text User when reading non-fiction, it is first useful to unpick what knowledge is necessary to enable a reader to become a Text Participant. Non-fiction is a broad term: it encompasses everything that is not fiction, as the name suggests. As Gamble (2008, p74) points out, *perhaps it strikes you as strange that books are categorised according to what they are not* – or perhaps this thought had not occurred to you before!

Activity

Think about the role of Text Participant in Freebody and Luke's (1990) model.

Text Participant

- Develop personal resources to make meaning possible – comprehension strategies
- Understand genre/text convention

- What personal resources are needed to make meaning possible when reading an information or reference text? Are they the same as those needed to read a procedural text such as a recipe or technical manual?
- How can you ensure you have a full understanding of the generic and text conventions needed to read the full range of non-fiction? Identify scholarly articles and resources that will help you.

As previously stated, it is important to understand that these four roles are interrelated and interdependent for a successful reader. However, it is occasionally useful to spend some time explicitly teaching children how to assume each of the roles in order to ensure they can move fluidly between them as and when necessary to read for meaning and enjoyment.

Teaching your class: Year 3

In Year 3 the focus moves from learning to read to reading to learn, and children should be able to access texts independently, although some may still need guidance and advice when tackling unfamiliar words. This lesson would be most effectively taught in a library environment, either within the school or in a community library; if this is not possible it will be necessary to collect together a large number of reference books. Not all of them need to be relevant to the topic, but some must include the necessary information for the task.

Context

This Year 3 class are generally secure in their understanding of grapho-phonic cues; they have already been involved in *Talk for Writing* activities (see **www.talk4writing. co.uk** for details) to familiarise themselves with the key features of information texts such as contents lists, index, alphabetic ordering, etc. They have a basic understanding of a range of non-fiction text types and their key purposes. Sue Palmer has developed a range of writing skeletons to help underpin children's understanding of different types of writing: see the further reading section at the end of this chapter for details.

Learning objectives

- To apply understanding of the conventions of non-fiction texts to access information.
- To use different reading strategies to retrieve information.
- To make appropriate choices about
  - the usefulness of texts for particular purposes;
  - ways of recording information for a peer-group audience.

Commentary

The main intention of these objectives is to provide the teacher with an opportunity to inspire and motivate active learning. This is in part based on the work of Kieran Egan (1942–), an educational professor and researcher with a particular interest in Vygotskian approaches; in his book The Educated Mind: How Cognitive Tools Shape Our Understanding *(1997) he outlined an alternative conception of educational development, different to a Piagetian or progressive models. Egan posits that the primary age phase is underpinned by the use of 'Tools of Oral Language', what he calls 'Mythic Understanding'. As part of this is a fascination with 'Puzzles and a Sense of Mystery', and this lesson is designed to allow children to use their reading skills to figure out pieces of the puzzle. For more information about Egan's theories of child development and resources to support planning and teaching go to the Imaginative Education Research Group website* **http://ierg.ca.**

Introduction to the lesson

Before the children enter the room place a series of objects on their tables, in this case artefacts from the term's history topic on the Iron Age, but it would work equally well with a series of random objects. When they come in to the lesson give them two minutes to look at, handle and discuss the item on their table. Ask them to jot down any key descriptive words or guesses about the name or purpose of the object on mini whiteboards.

Tell the children that you don't know for definite what they are – they were just something you 'found' in the cupboard – and ask for ideas for how you could find out. Let the children use talk partners to come up with suggestions. They may suggest asking someone else, an internet search or looking it up in a book (or other things adults wouldn't think of!).

Commentary

Not all lessons have to start out as a whole group, and learning objectives can be shared as the lesson progresses. (However, if it is your school's policy to start each lesson with an explicit learning objective, then they can be introduced and displayed at the start, but do it before the children start handling the artefacts.) This can help maintain the 'Mystery', but it is doubly important to use plenaries to ensure the learning has been explicitly understood.

Main lesson

Introduction

Using a general reference book, such as an encyclopaedia, model using the alphabet or the index to look up some of the guesses to 'see if the artefact is in there' (the feature used will depend on the structure of the book: a true encyclopaedia is one big index so has no need of another!). It is important *not* to find the answer yet.

> ## Commentary
>
> *In order to develop resilience as a text user the children need to see that the right answer sometimes isn't in the first place they look. Part of the modelling being done by the teacher is about how to persevere when an answer is not immediately forthcoming.*

Explain to the children that they need to research the artefacts and find the answers for themselves, and that these will form the basis of a class display. By the end of the lesson, they are going to be the resident expert on their artefact and they have to present the information in some way for the rest of the class. This can be written, drawn and labelled, done as a diagram, however they choose, but it must be on one side of A4 only.

> ## Commentary
>
> *It is important that the children are not given a choice for this activity and that they have to research the artefact on their table. If the area of study is unfamiliar to them, it adds unnecessary stress if they have to decide on a topic area; if they already have some knowledge they will often want to pick something they already know about. In order to help them understand the need to be able to access a range of texts quickly and appropriately the topic needs to be provided by the teacher. Do not allow children to change topic: if they are struggling to find information it will provide a learning and assessment opportunity for the teacher, who can suggest strategies.* (Have you checked the contents list? What about the index? What terms are you putting into the search engine: are they focused or specific enough?)

Show them the resources available to them: a full range of reference books and the computer or a tablet (but limit the time allowed on here to focus the search, for example no longer than two minutes per artefact). If you are in the library you need to be near the history section and may have to explain how the library shelves are organised, but remember this is about solving a puzzle so don't make it too easy! At this point give each child a query card (you should make four to a piece of A4):

Name:	Name:
?	?
Name:	Name:
?	?

Figure 6.3 Query card

If children get stuck, they can bring the teacher/adults in the classroom the query card (if they are proficient writers they can be encouraged to write their query, leaving room for any others later in the lesson; if their writing needs support then the teacher can scribe the problem). This acts as a record of the interventions and guidance received: it can be ticked off as queries are answered. It might be as simple as *Where do I find the contents page?* or as difficult as *Where do I start?*

Then start them off on the research! If anyone needs stretching or completes their information gathering and recording quickly, ask them to try and establish what the artefacts have in common, i.e. they come from the same time period.

Plenary

Have a display board or space ready for the results of their research and put them up immediately. Ask the children to reflect on which strategies made the research easier, and identify one or two children who can describe how they overcame a problem or query to get to an answer.

Commentary

While the topic for research can support another curriculum area it is important to emphasise the learning in terms of reading: what skills have they applied? How did it help them? The display will act as a catalyst for lessons in the other curriculum area, but the explicit understanding of how reference books can help us find out things will be lost if the plenary discussion is about what they discovered rather than how.

Assessment (measuring achievement)

Assessment for learning
- The plenary discussion at the end of the lesson provides a good way of allowing for self-reflection. Children are often very good at identifying the next steps they need

to take as individuals, so as a final activity you could have a number of statements placed around the teaching space linked to effective research reading (e.g. *I need to practise using an index; I need to learn how to skim read quickly for meaning; I want to learn how to scan for specific key words*) and ask the children to stand near the one they feel appropriate for them. Names can be jotted on the statement and used to inform planning of guided reading activities.

Assessment at the point of learning

- The query cards offer the children an opportunity to identify the barriers they are facing at the point of learning; they also provide a record for the teacher. However, it is important to observe, question and discuss as the research is happening, as not every child will hit a barrier they feel they need help with but may use problem-solving literacy skills independently or with peer support. Be aware of the need to look for this.

Assessment of learning

- The accuracy and coherence of the display, as well as the appropriateness of the mode chosen (diagram; summary paragraph; illustration) will indicate the success of the research and the children's ability to apply learnt skills independently.

Challenges

- A lack of appropriate resources and reference books can make a lesson like this difficult to manage. Ideally, a fully equipped library will be on hand, but for many rural schools (and some town/city ones!) this can be an issue. Local libraries often offer a schools' service and it is worth talking to the librarian to see if books can be brought in from across the region to support the lesson.

- Children's overreliance on internet search engines to provide 'easy' answers can stop them looking for the most accurate or detailed information. Scaffolds in the form of a list of useful websites can focus them on the task at hand: the websites themselves are texts that are structured in different ways, so are actually more useful than a random search.

Application of learning

Links to other areas of the curriculum

This sort of investigative approach can be applied across the curriculum. It can be used to explore how levers work in design and technology; to find the meaning of key science vocabulary; to discover about the life and work of an artist or musician. The possibilities are endless!

Next lesson

Build upon the next steps identified by the children in the assessment for learning and ensure they are addressed. Guided reading can be used to address the teaching of particular reading strategies and conventions of reference texts; book-talk opportunities, where children can share a range of text types they have found that interest them, will also encourage them to engage with non-fiction.

As a point to note, the National Curriculum (DfE, 2013) objective of reading texts that are structured in different ways can be extended to encompass non-traditional narratives such as *The Mysteries of Harris Burdick* by Chris Van Allsburg, *Voices in the Park* by Anthony Browne, *The Invention of Hugo Cabret* by Brian Selznick or *Charlie Cook's Favourite Book* by Julia Donaldson. The more opportunity children are given to access unusual books that play with convention, the more they will be inspired to explore.

Learning outcomes review

It should be clear how the children need to be given opportunity to take on the four roles of a successful reader in order to be able to use texts independently for the purpose they were intended. They need to build upon early work as *Code-Breakers* to become *Participants, Users* and *Analysers* of the text; but it is important to understand that these roles are not linear and can be developed concurrently. As a teacher it is your role to enable the development of an independent reader (the role of the enabling adult is explained more in Chapter 8 of this book).

Further reading

www.suepalmer.co.uk/education_publications_skeletons.php

Sue Palmer has developed a range of resources to support literacy development, including a series of writing skeletons that help children visualise the structure of different types of text. Very useful as a starting point to help early understanding of generic convention.

Waugh, D and Jolliffe, W (2013) *English 5–11: A Guide for Teachers*. London: Routledge.

A comprehensive text that provides lesson ideas linked to UK year groups and age phases. Chapter 9 of this edition is about Reading and Writing for Information.

References

Department for Education (DfE) (2013) *The National Curriculum in England: Framework Document*. London: DfE.

Freebody, P and Luke, A (1990) Literacies programs: debates and demands in cultural context. *Prospect* (an Australian journal of TESOL), 5 (3): 7–16.

Gamble, N (2008) More than information: engaging hearts and minds with non-fiction, in Goodwin, P (ed.) *Understanding Children's Books: A Guide for Education Professionals*. London: Sage.

Janks, H (2014) *Doing Critical Literacy: Texts and Activities for Students and Teachers*. London: Routledge.

Chapter 7

Year 4: Identifying themes

Learning outcomes

Being able to identify themes in a text is a skill that will be increasingly used throughout school. But it is also how we become critically literate as readers. This means children are less vulnerable to hidden messages and curricula which may reinforce stereotypes and values that do not match those of contemporary society.

This chapter will allow you to achieve the following outcomes:

- know how to structure and scaffold a literary investigation;
- understand what a theme is in relation to plot, topic or moral;
- develop an understanding of critical literacy and its importance for learners.

Teachers' Standards

Working through this chapter will help you meet the following standards:

2. Promote good progress and outcomes by pupils.
3. Demonstrate good subject and curriculum knowledge.
4. Plan and teach well-structured lessons.

Links to the National Curriculum

Years 3 and 4 programme of study

READING – Comprehension
Pupils should be taught to:

- develop positive attitudes to reading and understanding of what they read by:

  ✓ identifying themes and conventions in a wide range of books

- understand what they read, in books they can read independently, by:

  ✓ identifying main ideas drawn from more than one paragraph and summarising these
  ✓ identifying how language, structure, and presentation contribute to meaning.

(DfE, 2013)

Key focus: Developing critical literacy

Being critically literate means doing more than just reading for meaning. It is about becoming aware of the myriad of social, moral, cultural and political influences present in texts, even those for very young children. It is underpinned by a willingness to question and to challenge received wisdom: in terms of reading, it is about identifying the choices made by the writer *as well as* identifying why the choices may have been made. Critical literacy, at its heart, allows the reader to expose the assumptions and bias of the writer in order to make a conscious choice about how to respond.

Much of the pedagogical application is based on the work of Paulo Freire, who observed that *the cognitive dimensions of the literacy process must include the relationships of men with their world* (Freire, 1985, p50). This idea is reflected in the current National Curriculum (DfE, 2013, p4), where the introduction to the Reading programmes of study states: *Good comprehension draws from linguistic knowledge (in particular of vocabulary and grammar) and on knowledge of the world.*

How then do we encourage children to develop a knowledge of the world that is wider than their personal experience? Reading a wide range of fiction and non-fiction can help, but if we are to use literature to help children develop an understanding of the world in which we live we also have to acknowledge that these texts are written to describe the world as it is seen, experienced and imagined by the writer.

Activity

Even non-fiction is presented in a particular way by the writer/illustrator which may influence how it is intended to be read. Consider the following images (Figure 7.1):

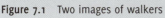

Figure 7.1   Two images of walkers

(Continued)

(Continued)

Both images show walkers on the Welsh Coastal Path during the summer.

- Which image is likely to be chosen for a holiday brochure?
- Which would be used for a travel blog?
- Which is most likely to appeal to a local tourist information office for a promotional poster?
- Why would the author/designer of each text reject the other photo?

It doesn't really matter if you chose the same photo for all texts: you will have made a series of decisions based on the perceived audience and purpose. Think about what decisions you made and what influenced your choice.

In order to help children understand how texts are shaped by their author you must teach them how to interrogate the text. Children are naturally inquisitive: they will have lots of questions, and this can easily be extended to questions beyond the literal and obvious (this links to Bloom's taxonomy as discussed in Chapter 3). Hilary Janks (2010) makes reference to four interdependent orientations which need to be explored in a *Synthesis Model of Critical Literacy* which can be represented as shown in Figure 7.2.

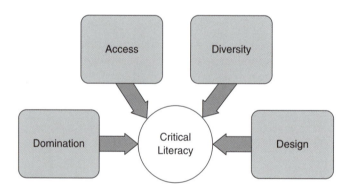

Figure 7.2 Synthesis Model of Critical Literacy

Activity

Think about the four orientations identified by Janks (2010) (Table 7.1).

- What do the terms 'domination', 'access', 'diversity' and 'design' mean in relation to children's literature?
- How might each be used to prevent children from being engaged by a text?

Table 7.1 Four orientations

Orientation	Possible barrier to reading
Domination	e.g. Constant use of gendered pronouns (for example 'he') may alienate girls or imply male dominance
Access	
Diversity	
Design	

Topic or theme?

Subject-specific vocabulary can often be used correctly even though the speaker or writer would find it difficult to explain: we are often uncritical of our language choices, assuming that those around us share our understanding of common words. As a teacher you will often find yourself being asked to define basic literacy terms so it is important to be clear on their meanings. It is very difficult to unpick and address misunderstandings if you are not able to articulate key vocabulary and help children differentiate between words that are often used synonymously.

Activity

A quick internet search brings several definitions for the word 'theme'. Read the following and think about how they might cause confusion:

By theme here we mean not a message – a word no good writer likes applied to his work – but the general subject, as the theme of an evening of debates may be World Wide Inflation.

(credited to writer John Gardner)

The theme is the container for your story. Theme will attempt to hold all the elements of your story in place. It is like a cup. A vessel. A goblet. The plot and characters and dialogue and setting and voice and everything else are all shaped by the vessel.

(by Terry Bain in Chapter 9 of the Gotham Writers' Workshop's book *Writing Fiction: The Practical Guide from New York's Acclaimed Creative Writing School*, published by Bloomsbury)

Themes can be divided into two categories: a work's thematic concept is what readers 'think the work is about' and its thematic statement being 'what the work says about the subject'.

(Wikipedia citation of Griffith, Kelley (2010) *Writing Essays about Literature* (8th edn.), published by Cengage Learning)

In *Exploring Children's Literature,* Gamble (2013) acknowledges that the words 'subject' and 'theme' are both used to describe what a story is about, but their difference is also emphasised. She describes subject as being more of a description of the key character and events (a young hero's quest to find a golden fleece), whereas the theme is a *central unifying idea* (the meaning of courage; overcoming adversity).

Teaching your class: Year 4

By the end of Year 4 the children should be increasingly independent in their ability to express their ideas and justify their views. They should also be gaining confidence in recording those views accurately. By providing them with an investigation rather than a series of questions to answer you can enable and encourage their independence, although it is still important to model and scaffold key strategies for accessing texts.

Using picture books with readers that are chronologically older than the target audience you can draw upon multimodal cues to aid critical literacy; it also helps the children understand that themes are not tied up in complicated texts or complex use of language. For this lesson I will refer to *Cave Baby* by Julia Donaldson and illustrated by Emily Gravett; *Not on a School Night* by Rebecca Patterson; and *Not Now, Bernard* by David McKee. However, the lesson ideas will work equally well with selections of poetry or novels once the principle of identifying a theme is understood.

Context

The children in this Year 4 class experience a wide range of literature. They are read to regularly and encouraged to choose their own reading material. Book talk is a regular feature of their classroom, both to encourage familiarity with texts and to provide underpinning for their writing.

Learning objectives

- To identify the key themes which link a group of texts.

- To understand how the themes are different to the subject of the texts.

- To be able to justify their views and provide evidence from the text to support their ideas.

Commentary

In Chapter 6 we discussed how Freebody and Luke (1990) identified four related roles undertaken by the reader: Code-Breaker, Participant, User and Analyst. This lesson particularly focuses on the role of Analyst, defined by Janks (2011) as when the reader pays attention to the social effects of texts.

Introduction to the lesson

The Full Picture: choose two or three digital images and crop them to show just one section of the picture. Print off the cropped section in colour (if appropriate) and give copies to the children to discuss the following questions in pairs/threes:

- Who is in the picture?

- What are they doing?

- Where do you think they are?

For example, give the children this image first (Figure 7.3):

Figure 7.3 Two walkers: close up

After two minutes show them the original photo (Figure 7.4):

Figure 7.4 Two walkers: long shot

How does this change their answers?

For some groups you might choose not to crop the picture; instead you can give them an image that contains an unusual backdrop or angle not normally seen of a famous landmark (see Figure 7.5), but the questions will be the same.

Figure 7.5 London pavement

Discuss how elements of the image can be taken out of context to create a different 'story': perhaps this is not the 2012 London Olympics, and instead the group of young people are being chased by an alien! Would it be so easy to identify the place if Nelson's column or the taxi were removed from the picture?

Commentary

It is important to recognise that some children may lack the experience and knowledge of the world, even in their own country, to recognise the significance of these iconic images, so choose the pictures you will use wisely. It is necessary to give them copies of the first image to allow the children to study it up close for details, but in the case of the cropped image the full reveal can be done on a projector or interactive whiteboard.

Highlight for the children the idea that things are not always what they seem: even a photograph can be taken in such a way that the full 'picture' is not visible, and that it is important to be aware that things might be hidden from the viewer.

Main lesson

Introduction

Tell the children that today they are going to be text detectives. Share the learning objectives with them; also share your definition of 'themes' and 'subject' in relation to the text.

Commentary

It would be useful to have your definitions for key subject vocabulary displayed somewhere throughout this lesson: if it is not possible to have it constantly visible on the whiteboard, then provide it as laminated cards on tables for reference. This will enable children to check for themselves if they feel they have accurately identified a theme that meets the agreed criteria.

Hand out copies of *Cave Baby*, *Not Now, Bernard* and *Not on a School Night* to groups of four and give them five minutes to familiarise themselves with the stories. Then model looking at the front cover of the book to identify the different modes used by the author.

Commentary

This should not be done as a shared activity: it is important that the children see how you spot the clues in the text and start to analyse them. Some of the features you could look at include the following:

- *Font: you can pick out how* Cave Baby *is written differently at the bottom to the rest of the text because it is written the way you would expect to see it on the front of that book. The writer/publisher wants you to recognise it.*

- *Picture: how does it give us clues about what might come next? The drawing is definitely a mammoth and not an elephant, you can tell by the way the ears are drawn: elephants' ears are much bigger.*

- *Possible theme: childhood? The main character looks pretty young. Friendship? The mammoth and the baby are smiling at each other. Make it clear that you would have to read the rest of the book to check if your ideas are correct, and that this is the job of the class!*

This activity should be short, focused and once you feel the children understand how you are scanning and analysing the text you should let them take over their own investigation.

A frame can be provided to scaffold note-taking during this activity (Table 7.2).

Table 7.2 Taking notes for activity

	Cave Baby	Not Now, Bernard	Not on a School Night
Subject of the text:			
Theme 1: Evidence:			
Theme 2: Evidence:			
Theme 3: Evidence:			

Plenary

Ask a spokesperson from each group to feed back on one theme they have identified. Was it the same in all three texts? Give them time to explain how they reached their conclusion.

Key follow-up questions could be explored, e.g. one of the key themes that crosses all three stories is Parenthood/Parenting: did the children identify this? Is it presented the same way in all three? How does the writer/illustrator want us to feel about parenting in *Not Now, Bernard?* What about in *Not on a School Night?*

In *Not Now, Bernard* and *Cave Baby* a shared theme could be identified as Loneliness: what evidence is there in the drawings to suggest this?

Finally, do a shared writing activity to finish this sentence:

Today we learnt …

Commentary

This lesson is an early step in becoming a truly critical reader and text analyst. Some of the strategies will have been used earlier in the children's education, and should be revisited regularly to build up their understanding as they become more experienced about the world. Therefore, it is important not to see this as a one-off lesson: it is part of a sequence to enable the children to become socially, morally, emotionally and politically aware.

Assessment (measuring achievement)

Assessment for learning
- Observation and careful monitoring of the discussions in the initial activity and main part of the lesson will highlight any limitations to the children's experience

or vocabulary that might act as a barrier to learning. Use this information to provide scaffolds and resources at the point of need, but also think about how this information can inform future planning: maybe more needs to be done to widen their awareness of the world outside their local environment, for example.

Assessment at the point of learning

- The children need to be familiar with text marking, annotation and scanning for specific information. Can they select evidence from the text appropriately or do they highlight long sections of the text? Are they able to articulate words and phrases that identify the theme? If children are able to be selective it means they understand how to identify evidence from the text appropriately.

- If the children are highlighting/identifying chunks of text rather than words and phrases, guide them through the process by asking questions: are there any key words or elements of the image that they think are more important in identifying the theme? Look at each sentence in turn: is every word necessary as evidence? Do they all link to the same theme? Is the layout suggesting anything to them as readers? Help the children see how quality of evidence, not quantity, is important in this sort of investigation.

Assessment of learning

- Summative assessment about the children's understanding can be made using the children's notes and annotations. This can be done on the frame provided, or on sticky notes, or sections of the text can be photocopied to enable the children to write on it.

- The writing ability of the child must be taken into account here, as must any support provided during the activity. It is not a spelling test, so there is no need to link support for spelling to ability to read critically: what is important is the children's ability to summarise and justify ideas.

Challenges

- Often, when judging reading comprehension, children's ability to articulate more complex themes and ideas is held back by the limitations of their own vocabulary. As was stated in Chapter 3, increased vocabulary leads to improved reading comprehension (Clarke *et al.*, 2010; Gough and Tunmer, 1986; Nation, 2005; National Reading Panel, 2000), so it is important we enable the development of an appropriate vocabulary. Providing a dictionary/thesaurus and encouraging children to look up alternative words for accuracy can help address this, but only if children have the skills to use these tools effectively.

- Cultural diversity may mean some classes need more help than others in identifying particular themes. The way different cultures demonstrate Respect, for example, may not be immediately obvious to some children, and so the cultural context of the class and the chosen texts needs to be considered. This is particularly relevant in historical fiction where, as Gamble (2013) points out, the cultural origin will be reflected in the text, but this may only provide one perspective of many and may affect the themes presented.

Application of learning

Links to other areas of the curriculum
There are obvious links to personal, social and health education in terms of the themes explored and these could be raised for discussion during circle time. However, critical literacy and the ability to identify themes, ideology and sub-texts are valuable across the curriculum and have real life application.

Next lesson

Plan for regular investigations, for example use author studies to explore if certain authors return to particular themes. Encourage text marking and annotation in a range of lessons (again, sticky notes are very handy where class sets of books are too expensive to replace due to being written on!), particularly in subject areas where evidence can be gleaned from the text.

Learning outcomes review

You should now have an understanding of how critical literacy and text analysis can be developed with readers. The concepts of theme and subject, and the difference between these terms, should be clear. It should also be clear that it is important to secure your own understanding of key terminology in order to effectively teach conceptual understanding with clarity: attention to your own wider reading and scholarly activity will help you become confident and competent in the classroom.

Further reading

Two of the texts drawn upon in this chapter are particularly useful and to be recommended as further reading to support your subject knowledge development:

Gamble, N (2013) *Exploring Children's Literature: Reading with Pleasure and Purpose* (3rd edn.). London: Sage.

This provides ideas for teaching as well as an explanation of key aspects of literature.

Janks, H (2011) *Doing Critical Literacy: Texts and Activities for Students and Teachers.* London: Routledge.

Although this is a text aimed at teachers of young people and adults, it is very useful if you want to understand how literacy is affected by power relationships, as well as how texts act on and position the reader. Janks' other text, *Literacy and Power* (2010), is also very insightful.

Another useful text for exploring how texts can be used to influence readers is:

Hollindale, P (1988) *Ideology and the Children's Book.* Stroud: Thimble Press.

This is a short pamphlet, but probably one of the most valuable reads for those who are wondering why critical literacy is important for even early readers.

References

Clarke, PJ, Snowling, MJ, Truelove, E and Hulme, C (2010) Ameliorating children's reading comprehension difficulties: a randomized control trial. *Psychological Science*, 20: 1–11.

Department for Education (DfE) (2013) *The National Curriculum in England: Framework Document.* London: DfE.

Donaldson, J (2010) *Cave Baby.* London: Macmillan.

Freebody, P and Luke, A (1990) Literacies programs: debates and demands in cultural context. *Prospect* (an Australian journal of TESOL), 5 (3): 7–16.

Freire, P (1985) *The Politics of Education: Culture, Power, and Liberation.* Westport, CT: Bergin and Garvey.

Gamble, N (2013) *Exploring Children's Literature: Reading with Pleasure and Purpose* (3rd edn.). London: Sage.

Gough, PB and Tumner, WE (1986) Decoding, reading and reading disability. *Remedial and Special Education*, 7: 6–10.

Janks, H (2010) *Literacy and Power.* London: Routledge.

Janks, H (2014) *Doing Critical Literacy: Texts and Activities for Students and Teachers.* London: Routledge.

McKee, D (1980) *Not Now, Bernard.* London: Andersen Press.

Nation, K (2005) Reading comprehension difficulties, in Snowling, MJ and Hulme, C (eds.) *The Science of Reading.* Oxford: Blackwell, pp248–65.

National Reading Panel (2000) *Teaching Children to Read: An Evidence-Based Assessment of the Scientific Literature on Reading and Its Implications for Reading Instruction.* Washington DC: National Institute of Child Health and Human Development.

Patterson, R (2012) *Not on a School Night.* London: Macmillan.

Chapter 8

Year 4: Playing with plays

Learning outcomes

Drama is an important part of our social and cultural development, and as such is embedded into the curriculum for English. However, the art of reading a script and understanding the way it mediates between writer, actor and audience is often overlooked. Even very young children can take part in performance, and it is possible to teach them how a written text becomes a performance text through script reading quite easily.

This chapter will allow you to achieve the following outcomes:

- know the conventions of basic script-writing and how they impact on the reader;
- understand the difference between the reader of the script and the 'reader' of the play.

Teachers' Standards

Working through this chapter will help you meet the following standards:

2. Promote good progress and outcomes by pupils.
3. Demonstrate good subject and curriculum knowledge.
4. Plan and teach well-structured lessons.
6. Make accurate and productive use of assessment.

Links to the National Curriculum

Years 3 and 4 programme of study

READING – Comprehension
Pupils should be taught to:

- develop positive attitudes to reading and understanding of what they read by:

  ✓ preparing poems and play scripts to read aloud and to perform, showing understanding through intonation, tone, volume and action

- understand what they read, in books they can read independently, by:

  ✓ drawing inferences such as inferring characters' feelings, thoughts and motives from their actions, and justifying inferences with evidence.

(DfE, 2013)

Key focus: Reading to perform

Scripts are often used to support the teaching of writing rather than as a text for reading. The text is locked down, used as a model for layout and structure rather than enjoyed as a pathway to performance. While it is important that children understand the conventions of script-writing, it is equally important that they experience reading scripts and plays for performance purposes, in other words using the text for the purpose it was written.

> *Reading plays has much in common with reading musical scores; and yet, what score is designed to be read, like a printed play, for enjoyment, as an end in itself?*

(Meisel, 2007, p1)

In order to read a play in script form it is important to understand how the conventions of the text support the intended reader *and* the intended audience; it is also important to understand how the reader as performer needs to be able to use empathy as a reading skill in order to bring the text to life with some success. Children need to be taught how to access a script as a whole text, but they also need experience of reading to perform if they are to understand how script differs from prose in any meaningful sense.

The key issue holding back effective drama pedagogy, of which script reading is a feature, is a lack of confidence by teaching staff. This was identified by Neelands (2008) as *a degree of professional insecurity*, even among those employed to teach drama as a discrete subject in a secondary school context. The reduction in explicit objectives linked to drama in the National Curriculum (DfE, 2013) could be seen as further evidence of a reduction in the need for expertise in drama as a tool and as a subject, but it must be noted that it is still a statutory feature: the debate should be around quality of drama teaching and subject knowledge, not quantity.

Drama is more often linked with secondary school teaching and thus much of the subject-specific guidance is directed towards teachers working with the 11+ age range. Materials for primary schools are often more focused on activities to do with the children rather than understanding the theoretical underpinning. This can make it feel difficult for primary teachers to gather the knowledge and understanding to fully support children in this area.

Activity

Conduct an audit of your own issues and challenges in terms of subject knowledge (Table 8.1).

Table 8.1 Issues and challenges

Issue or challenge	Is this an issue for me or the wider school?
I am/we are confident about using a variety of drama techniques.	
I/we understand drama to be much more than the 'presentation' of scripts, improvised ideas or the use of roles.	
I/we allocate sufficient time to the structured, interactive drama approaches within units of work linked to the development of reading and writing skills.	
I/we select challenging texts and associated drama activities in order to provide opportunities for the development of critical thinking and deep/profound learning.	
I/we ensure there is focus on learning, understanding and assessing drama across speaking and listening, reading and writing units of work.	
I/we have had sufficient professional development on planning, teaching, evaluating and assessing drama within English, supported by current high-quality resources and professional support.	
I/we have a good understanding of drama education in the primary phase and I/we are aware of the progression in drama throughout the full compulsory school age range.	

(Adapted from *Developing Drama in English: A Handbook for English Subject Leaders and Teacher*, DfE, 2010)

Now identify at least three scholarly sources that will enable you to address these issues.

N.B. you will notice the audit asks you to identify if the issue is personal or one for the school: it is important to realise some aspects need to be addressed as part of a wider school ethos and knowledge base, but once identified it is equally important to raise it with your colleagues.

Who is the reader?

A script is actually written for multiple readers as well as a pretend audience: the playwright is rarely in a position to interact with the watchers of the play and has to rely on the understanding of the actors involved to transmit the actions, emotions and motivations of the characters through their performance of the dialogue. Other, non-spoken aspects of the text, in the form of stage directions, help this process along. Meisel (2007) credits George Bernard Shaw with the changing convention of stage direction in script-writing: in order to make his plays appeal to a wider readership, and generate interest in them, he made the non-dialogue as interesting as the dialogue. Thus, stage directions changed from technical advice to descriptive prose that detailed exactly the author's intention, and often that is what is taught to children now. However, not all scripts contain such prescriptive advice as the adverbials intended to guide every action of the actor, and it is important that the children are given opportunities to read, digest and then make decisions based on what is not in the script as well as what is.

Activity

Think about the different job roles associated with putting on a performance, for example:

- Actor
- Director
- Technical Support (lighting/sound)
- Costumier.

Are there aspects of a script that are specifically written for each of these people? Using an example script, look for evidence that the writer had these roles in mind when constructing the text. How many different implied readers are there in your example?

Reading as a social activity

More than any other medium, a play is a social endeavour: it should be read together by a minimum of the number of actors involved. However, too many readers at any one time is counter-productive. Many of the participants become passive onlookers unless given a role. Think of the way many school plays are rehearsed with a large number of children doing very little at any one time while the small number of actors involved in the dialogue practise their role and you will understand the scenario! However, it must also be noted that reading as a social practice in school is not always enabled as effectively as one might hope.

One of the key issues, highlighted by the United Kingdom Literacy Association (UKLA) 'Teachers as Readers' project (2006–08), is that teachers tend to control the reading taking place within the classroom (Cremin *et al.*, 2014). Talk about reading tended to be in the form of formal exchanges rather than between children making sense of the text for real-world purposes. Reading scripts can provide an opportunity for the teacher to step back from a position of control and move towards a more equitable reading experience for the children, which will encourage reading for pleasure in a meaningful sense. The link between script and dramatic narrative can thus be exploited:

> *Through drama children can live inside and create any story together! ... They can create, elaborate or change stories collectively using their bodies and emotions, as well as their minds.*

(CfSA, 2010)

An often underestimated barrier to reading for pleasure, particularly of scripts, is lack of access to appropriate resources. Plays written specifically for children to perform are not widely published in the same way that narratives written for children to read are produced. Reading schemes will often include a play script, but this will often not be based on something performed outside the classroom; scripts for plays attended by children are often based on adaptations of popular books and thus the readership may well be familiar with character, plot and story through the original (which can sometimes inadvertently scaffold their understanding and ability to interpret the text independently). However, it is still possible to find high-quality, real text versions which will introduce children to reading for performance in a purposeful way.

Activity

Audit the scripts available for readers in your classroom.

- Are there opportunities for readers to choose scripts for independent reading?
- Does your library contain scripts for children to read?

Think about ways you can enable children to read scripts outside of lesson time.

Teaching your class: Year 4

The current National Curriculum (2013) provides combined objectives for lower Key Stage 2, i.e. children aged 7–9. It is important to realise that many of the objectives will need to be unpicked to identify the progression in skills that make the learning different for each age group to avoid unnecessary repetition of tasks. The lesson outlined below is not intended to lead to script-writing, and it is not about becoming familiar with the conventions of script-writing, as this is likely to have been embedded as part of earlier teaching in this age phase. The lesson is focused on developing an understanding of character through reading comprehension.

Context

This Year 4 class have experienced turning sections of narrative prose into script. They have a good understanding of what a script should include and the purpose of these conventions, for example a cast list to identify number of players; basic stage directions; the name of the speaker on the left/dialogue on the right.

The class will work in small groups dictated by the number of cast involved in each scene they are given.

At this stage you will notice there is no specific text being suggested. This is because the selection of appropriate scripts will depend largely on the resources you have available: if you have whole-class sets of a script then by all means utilise them, but if not then a helpful source is the BBC website, which provides links to a series of radio, television and film scripts at **www.bbc.co.uk/writersroom/scripts/search?genre= childrens&platform=tv&orderby=recent**.

The children's scripts are largely based around CBeebies and CBBC programmes that may well be familiar to the children, so you will need to encourage them to think about how they want to interpret the characters and events.

Learning objectives

- To infer a character's feelings, thoughts and motives from the dialogue in a script and demonstrate how this affects the character's actions.

- To use the voice in performance, adjusting volume and pace to perform effectively.

- To demonstrate understanding of character through appropriate use of intonation.

Commentary

It is important to keep the focus on reading comprehension and emphasise how the script can help us understand character. In order to successfully perform a role the children will need to empathise with their character, so when sharing the objectives it is helpful to do a strategy check with them to remind them what empathy is.

Empathy is different to sympathy: we can understand and sympathise with others, but empathy requires us to put ourselves in their shoes, to think about how the events might affect the way they feel inside and to begin to experience it for ourselves. Perkins (2008, p29) states that a good book for young children is one with which they can make an emotional link, *but this can sometimes be difficult if the text is being mediated by a more expert or adult reader. By reading, discussing characters and their motivations and then performing, the children will be supported by each other in understanding how to become, and thus empathise with, someone else.*

Introduction to the lesson

Nothing more than feelings: in pairs or small groups give the children a pack of cards, face down, with a series of emotions written on them (see suggestions in Figure 8.1). Each child takes turns to choose a card, concealing it from the others, and make an appropriate facial expression: the partner/group then has to identify the word on the card. A tally of correctly guessed words can be kept, and if the class is particularly competitive then the number of correct guesses in two minutes could be added up. (If the activity is being done as a timed competition it is important that ground rules are established first, e.g. number of guesses allowed, etc.).

Happy	Bored	Distraught
Ecstatic	Sad	Wistful
Thoughtful	Content	Dejected
Weary	Melancholic	Blissful

Figure 8.1 Emotion cards

Commentary

It is important to include a range of synonyms and alternative words in this activity. This will serve dual purposes: it will encourage children to extend their vocabulary range, and it will also help them understand that each word is not a simple substitute for another, it is a different shade of meaning. For example, 'distraught' is not just another way of saying 'sad', it is a particular kind of sadness and will affect the way we show it physically.

For the next round, choose a word, phrase or sentence (e.g. Hello/What's going on/And then it happened …) and write it on the board. This time, when the children pick a card they have to say this sentence in a way that indicates the emotion through their voice. N.B. by providing the words you are ensuring that tone, pitch and pace of voice are used to indicate emotion rather than word choice.

Select children to demonstrate some of the more difficult words, or ask groups/pairs to identify and share good examples by individuals.

Main lesson

Introduction

Share the learning objective with the children, emphasising the link between character and voice (which is underpinned by the previous activity). Introduce the play text to the class and explain that different sections of the text are going to be allocated for groups to read, annotate and perform by the end of the lesson. Devise success criteria together that will enable children to demonstrate they have learnt how to infer a character's thoughts, feelings and emotions: one example could be that annotations and stage directions written by the children will include adverbs and powerful verbs that are linked to emotions.

Group children in a number that matches the actors' scene you want them to read and perform. This means that some groups may only have two members, some may have more than three, but all should have spoken roles.

Commentary

This lesson requires the teacher to become what Chambers (1991) named the Enabling Adult (see Figure 8.2). In this case the text is selected by the teacher; however, over time the children can be encouraged to select their own scripts for performance once they understand the process of reading to infer, annotate to enhance and clarify understanding.

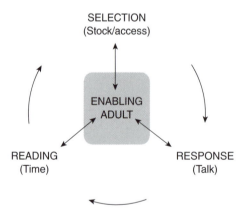

Figure 8.2 Based on Aidan Chambers' diagram of the reading circle (Chambers, 1991)

In order to engage and involve all the learners it is important to choose different scenes rather than have the whole class look at the same scene. This will allow for a meaningful discussion about the different interpretations of the same character in different scenarios; it encourages peer support as watching the performance does not lead to negative comparisons of 'good' interpretations and 'bad' ones. It also avoids the boredom of watching the same

---

set of events five or six different times! By allocating the sections of the script you can differentiate for reading ability, but beware of overly limiting less proficient readers: a mixed-ability approach will be far more beneficial to all, as the discussion will support understanding and still allow for proficient readers to articulate their ideas.

Finally, classroom layout and class size can make the task of organising performance feel daunting. The logistics of giving children space to read together, annotate and perform as an interwoven process rather than a series of steps means removing the desks at the beginning may be more effective than waiting until the performance element of the lesson. Reading does not have to happen at a desk, and children will arrange themselves accordingly.

Explain that by the end of the lesson each group will have performed their section of the text in such a way that the thoughts and emotions of the characters are clear to the audience. Each group will need to skim read the script first and allocate characters. Then they are to read the script aloud, getting up to act out bits as and when they are ready, and writing their own stage directions and annotations about the characters that will help them understand thoughts, feelings and motivations. If the texts are real books that are going to be used in future, sticky notes can be used to annotate (cut into strips to be used at the appropriate points in the text).

Now for the difficult part: give the children a time limit until performance (depending on the length of text, 10 to 15 minutes for annotation/discussion/rehearsal should be adequate) and then step back *and let them read*. Be there to answer questions, but beware of stepping in to offer direction: that is not the point of the exercise and should be avoided. Instead, if a group or actor is having difficulty, support their reading of the text using the principles of guided reading, helping them to unpick and infer the actions from the way the dialogue is presented. The word cards used in the introduction activity can act as scaffolds for annotations and stage directions.

Commentary

Although guided reading as a strategy has a particular teaching sequence which would not be appropriate in this lesson, the principles are based upon high-quality interactions between teacher and pupil and this means knowing when to intervene and how to intervene *(Gamble, 2013, p52). Think carefully about what reading strategies will be most useful in guiding the reading to encourage empathy and inference, rather than inferring or trying to explain the emotive response indicated in your opinion.*

Plenary

Once the time limit is up, prepare a performance space and allow the groups to perform in the order dictated by the script so a coherent narrative is built up. Avoid discussion between scenes: allow the performance to happen and encourage smooth transition between groups by agreeing the procedure from the start (*Once your performance has ended, I will count slowly to 10. The group needs to sit down quickly and silently; the next group needs to be ready by the time I get to 10.*).

Commentary

Performance time is important, but it can be tempting to interrupt to offer advice or highlight good practice. Try to avoid this: when we go to the theatre we don't interrupt a performance with our views, except in extreme circumstances!

Make notes of observations you want to make at the end, and encourage the audience to do the same: sticky notes can be put up afterwards to highlight 'Things we liked' or who met the success criteria and how, and this can then be displayed and discussed at the end of the performance.

Assessment (measuring achievement)

Assessment for learning
- The first activity will enable you to identify children who have a limited understanding of the range of emotions and how to express them. This can then be used to target adult support in the rest of the lesson. Again, it is important to remember that the teacher is not there to direct the performance, but you can model different ways of showing emotion through voice/action to aid understanding.

- During the main reading activity it is important to be available to answer questions, read unknown words for pronunciation, etc. to enable accurate understanding of the text.

Assessment at the point of learning
- The annotations and stage directions written by the children will offer an insight into their understanding of character. These can be photocopied in situ after the lesson if needed for recording purposes.

- Careful observation and listening to the groups' discussions will also indicate the children's understanding and ability to draw inference from the text.

Assessment of learning

- The performance itself will provide evidence of the children's ability to show understanding through intonation, tone, volume and action. The performance can be recorded if you want to review individual understanding; this can also be used for the children to self and peer review to encourage reflection and an awareness of their own needs and strengths.

Challenges

- Children's confidence can affect their willingness to perform: if you have a class where the social culture may make performance a challenge, getting one group to perform to another, rather than each group to the whole class, may make the actors feel safer. The key to success is familiarity: if drama in the classroom is a rare event, the children will feel more nervous about taking part. Don't let one experience of reluctance dictate how you implement the teaching; instead think about how you can ensure the classroom is a safe space for this kind of expression.

- Try not to see every reading experience as a direct lead to a writing task. This happens frequently with scripts, where they become models for the children's own script-writing or lead to a writing-in-role activity. Allow the performance to be the outcome: it is why the script was written in the first place!

Application of learning

Links to other areas of the curriculum

Empathy is a reading skill that will enable a better understanding of religious education and history in particular. Scripts can be chosen that link to key events in order to explore the human aspect, although it is very important that you make the distinction between what is a fictional account and what was really said. However, the same techniques can be applied to transcripts, for example allowing the children to read, annotate and perform Martin Luther King's *I have a dream* or Winston Churchill's wartime broadcasts before letting them listen to actual recordings: this should enable a greater understanding and insight of the words.

Next lesson

Encourage your class to reflect on how acting out the scene helped them understand the way the character was feeling or why they were acting in a particular way. Ask them to identify which strategies they found helpful: did the annotation support their understanding? Could it be applied to any other type of reading task?

Provide opportunities to read scripts in free-choice activities, and ensure space is available to allow for performance.

Learning outcomes review

It should now be clear that scripts can be used to support wider reading comprehension, and that the opportunity to use a script for its intended purpose is important if children are to see the point of the text. You should also feel confident in acting as an enabling adult and facilitator for learning. As long as the objective is clear and the success criteria agreed, the children can explore texts and then demonstrate their understanding to you in a range of ways; performance is just one of them.

The most important thing to ensure is access to high-quality texts for script reading: if you do not already have a range of scripts for use as classroom resources and as free reading activities then it is imperative you address this in your classroom environment.

Further reading

Baldwin, P (2008) *The Primary Drama Handbook*. London: Sage.

This book is signposted by National Drama in some of their materials. It contains a series of detailed drama lesson units to support learning, with a particular emphasis on narrative.

Department for Education (DfE) (2010) *Developing Drama in English: A Handbook for English Subject Leaders and Teachers*. London: DfE.

Although it is aimed at secondary teachers, this document provides good advice on planning for and monitoring learning through drama that will support teachers' understanding.

www.nationaldrama.org.uk

A useful subject body website to support teachers and drama organisations; there are links to publications and other resources to support subject knowledge development for practitioners.

References

Chambers, A (1991/2011 combined volume) *Tell Me: Children, Reading and Talk* and *The Reading Environment: How Adults Help Children Enjoy Books*. Woodchester: The Thimble Press.

Cremin, T, Mottram, M, Collins, FM, Powell, S and Safford, K (2014) *Building Communities of Engaged Readers: Reading for Pleasure.* London: Routledge.

CfSA (2010) *Drama: Using Stories.* Available at: **www.nationaldrama.org.uk**

Department for Education (DfE) (2013) *The National Curriculum in England: Framework Document.* London: DfE.

Gamble, N (2013) *Exploring Children's Literature: Reading with Pleasure and Purpose.* London: Sage.

Mciscl, M (2007) *How Plays Work: Reading and Performance.* Oxford: Oxford University Press.

Neelands, J (2008) *Drama: The Subject that Dare Not Speak Its Name.* Available at: **www.ite.org.uk**

Perkins, M (2008) Literature for the very young, in Goodwin, P (ed.) *Understanding Children's Books: A Guide for Education Professionals.* London: Sage.

Chapter 9

Year 5: Using drama with a class novel

Learning outcomes

This chapter explores how you can use drama strategies to actively plan for enhanced critical reading of text and the handling of abstract concepts such as opinion, stance and perspective.

This chapter will allow you to achieve the following outcomes:

- know how drama strategies can improve children's critical responses to text;
- develop an understanding of how explicit teacher commentary can support the children's development with analytical approaches;
- have a clear strategy for planning this through classroom activities.

Teachers' Standards

Working through this chapter will help you meet the following standards:

2. Promote good progress and outcomes by pupils.
3. Demonstrate good subject and curriculum knowledge.
4. Plan and teach well-structured lessons.
6. Make accurate and productive use of assessment.

Links to the National Curriculum

Year 5 programme of study

READING – Comprehension
Pupils should be taught to:

- maintain positive attitudes to reading and understanding what they read by:

    ✓ continuing to read and discuss an increasingly wide range of fiction, poetry, plays, non-fiction and reference books or textbooks
    ✓ reading books that are structured in different ways and reading for a range of purposes

- ✓ increasing their familiarity with a wide range of books, including myths, legends, and traditional stories, modern fiction, fiction from our literary heritage, and books from their cultures and traditions
- ✓ recommending books that they have read to their peers, giving reasons for their choices
- ✓ identifying and discussing themes and conventions in and across a wide range of writing
- ✓ making comparisons within and across books
- ✓ learning a wider range of poetry by heart
- ✓ preparing poems and plays to read aloud and to perform, showing understanding through intonation, tone and volume so that the meaning is clear to an audience

- understand what they read by:

  - ✓ checking that the book makes sense to them, discussing their understanding and exploring the meaning of words in context
  - ✓ asking questions to improve their understanding
  - ✓ drawing inferences such as inferring characters' feelings, thoughts and motives from their actions, and justifying inferences with evidence
  - ✓ predicting what might happen from details stated and implied
  - ✓ summarising the main ideas drawn from more than one paragraph, identifying key details that support the main ideas
  - ✓ identifying how language, structure and presentation contribute to meaning

- discuss and evaluate how authors use language, including figurative language, considering the impact on the reader
- distinguish between statements of fact and opinion
- retrieve, record and present information from non-fiction
- participate in discussions about books that are read to them and those they can read for themselves, building on their own and others' ideas and challenging views courteously
- explain and discuss their understanding of what they have read, including through formal presentations and debates, maintaining a focus on the topic and using notes where necessary
- provide reasoned justifications for their views.

(DfE, 2013)

Key focus: Using drama to facilitate collaborative learning and improved comprehension

Activity

Reflect on where drama features in your teaching to date. How do you use drama to support children explicitly with their reading development?

(Continued)

> *(Continued)*
>
> This will be useful for you to map your own relationship with drama, either from your own school experiences or as a teacher. How can drama engage children when working with a text and how is this harnessed to explicitly work on developing reading skills such as inference and deduction? Are children aware that this is what they are doing? Think about how this links to your understanding and planning for metacognitive approaches to learning.

Drama in the classroom enables both the children and the teacher to engage in a shared experience of reading and is often used as a creative approach to responding to and exploring texts. The idea of learning collaboratively is one that has been developed in many areas, not least through improving the quality of talk in the classroom (see Chapter 4). The value of collaboration and peer group discussions has been promoted to develop the ways in which teachers plan for and manage talk for learning (Alexander, 2004; Rojas-Drummond and Mercer, 2003). Mercer (2000) advocates that exploratory talk in the classroom will encourage children to engage critically and constructively with each other. In responding to the benefits of such talk, the effective use of drama to support learners can be a way of harnessing this talk in the exploration of a text. The interaction between the teacher and children within a well-structured drama activity is one that will promote ownership of the exploration with the children, promoting the idea that there can be a range of interpretations of text.

Despite being told that it is acceptable to have varied opinions and reactions to text, many children find this a difficult, sometimes even a 'scary', concept. What does a different interpretation look like? Does it matter if the teacher doesn't agree? How do they explain themselves? In structuring frequent and well-supported opportunities to talk about text with their peers, the teacher is being pro-active in ensuring that talk enhances the learning experience. Likewise, encouraging talk partners to consider their own questions about the text can be a powerful learning activity (Pressley, 2000). McGuinn (2014) suggests that effective use of teacher questioning will support the children in accessing the higher cognitive skills – all of which will promote the skills required to be a good critical reader: synthesis, analysis and evaluation. Neelands (1984) went on to suggest that there are seven areas of questioning which will support a teacher's commitment to collaborative learning, and these lend themselves to the use of drama in literacy which we will explore in this chapter. In particular, seeking information, provoking research, branching, seeking opinions and encouraging reflection are areas of exploratory drama work which are put forward in this chapter (Neelands, 1984).

The use of sculpting as a technique for building a first response to text allows the learners to engage and interact with each other and the text. Through careful questioning, the teacher can also manoeuvre the learning towards considering different perspectives. Such skills are often difficult to grasp as children move from a basic understanding towards a more conceptual interpretation. What do different readers think at this point in the narrative? What does the writer think and how did I arrive at that conclusion? What is a stance/perspective? Applying these considerations to a three-dimensional text in the middle of the room will allow children to look, consider, probe and reflect. They are no longer trying to find multiple meanings on a page, but working with peers to construct a living reflection of these interpretations by placing the reader and writer within the sculpted scene; a three-dimensional interpretation of a moment in time in the narrative. The activities outlined will facilitate conversations that help the children to construct meaning at the same time as owning the learning process. Throughout this process they will be collaborating within a learning community, working together to explore, empathise and expand ideas – the long-term gains allowing them to internalise these cognitive strategies (Ketch, 2005).

The optimal moments of learning described in the strategies below reflect the notion that *genres of language connected with dramatic action allow* conceptual *movement in and around imaginary worlds that are collectively and* actively *constructed in a social context* (Franks, 2015, p152). Over a number of years, I have seen children participating and growing in confidence within short time periods using these strategies. The impact on their critical reading of texts has been manifold and enabled me to work with a range of teachers and children to improve analytical reading (Beattie and Highfield, 2007). The opportunity to make clear links to writing threads through all of these activities and it is worth considering how these approaches can be explicitly linked to the writing which follows the reading of texts.

It is Hall's (2015) assertion that it is part of the human condition to want to engage with others in order to make meaning. The steady sequence of strategies to deepen children's thinking with these suggested drama activities enables them to *layer* meaning, *change* meaning and *adapt* meaning. The sense of empowerment alongside the development of difficult conceptual ideas maps the children's engagement and understanding of text, often taking them to a place of analytical consideration that would have eluded them if left to grapple with the text on the page.

Teaching your class: Year 5

The lesson below uses drama strategies to harness the interest and engagement of children as well as honing their comprehension skills. I have chosen *Journey to the River Sea* by Eva Ibbotson as this reaches out to children for a variety of reasons. The protagonist is a quiet, intelligent, determined young girl, Maia, who sets off on a journey to live with her only surviving family in South America. She is accompanied by the grim figure of her new governess who clearly has her own secrets. The children will read about the rainforest and all it has to offer in excitement and adventure with the same anticipation as Maia. They follow her physical and emotional journey as she is confronted with a less than welcoming family and tries to make sense of her new life. There is a range of characters who test Maia's strength of character, and the children are similarly confronted with spiteful cousins, unkind guardians, caring servants, a local boy with a hidden past, a runaway child actor and evil investigators. The appeal of the female protagonist with a tomboyish approach to the excitement of her new surroundings allows boys and girls to engage with her journey and watch as she forms close and loyal friendships with two young boys with troubles of their own. There is a thriller-like approach to the writing and the need to find out 'what happens next' is a motivating factor, coupled with the beautifully evocative descriptions of the rainforest and local town.

Context

The children in Year 5 have begun reading the opening chapters to *Journey to the River Sea*. They have spent some time examining their first meeting with Maia and considering how she will have felt upon hearing of the death of both of her parents. At this point, they have done a 'role on the wall' activity to record everything that they know about her and made some predictions about what the news of her distant relatives means, how she will manage and what might happen to her on her arrival in South America. These types of activities encourage an open approach to reading, particularly fiction, and allow the teacher to foster a safe learning environment in which they can encourage children to experiment with different ideas and scenarios.

The introduction of the character of the governess, Miss Minton, will also allow for some discussion about stereotypes based on her appearance and demeanour when talking to Maia. Children have very clear views on what they expect Miss Minton to be like as a person and are able to make predictions at this point about how she will be as a governess. These are worth revisiting as the novel progresses to reflect on preconceptions of character and also to examine how the narrative allows relationships to grow and change. Introductory work of this nature is not only a way into the text but also a means for providing meaningful material for reflection at a later date, encouraging the children to consider themselves as readers who react to the craft of a writer.

Some work can be done considering the way in which the Carter family are different to Maia, exploring how the characters and descriptions of the house contribute to a feeling of isolation.

Prior to the lesson, the children will need to familiarise themselves with the development in the narrative. Project the segment of text where we first meet Finn (Resource A, p99).

Resource A: page 99

But she did not at first recognise the boy who stood outside the hut, quietly waiting. He seemed to be the Indian boy who had taken her to Manaus, but his jet-black hair had gone, and so had the headband and the red paint. With his own fine, brown hair, he looked like any European boy who has lived a long time in the sun.

Except that he didn't. He looked like no boy Maia had ever seen, standing so still, not waving or shouting instructions, just being there.

Using 'role on the wall' as a means of exploring and collecting first thoughts, ask the children: *What do we learn about Finn? What are we able to infer about him beyond his physical features?* Ensure that you make it clear that first responses can be concrete answers using the text and that inferences will be an interpretation of text.

Resource B: page 99

The boy stretched out his hand and Maia jumped out.

'I've decided to trust you,' he said in English.

She had known really before he spoke. Now, she was sure.

Maia looked into his eyes. 'You can do that,' she said seriously. 'I wouldn't betray you to the crows – not for the world.'

'The crows … yes, that's the right name for them. So you know who I am?'

Now project Resource B and ask the children: *What else do we learn about Finn? What can we add to our understanding of Maia?* Explicitly talk about how, as the narrative moves forward, we can add to or change what we think about the text. This reiterates that they are in control of their responses to text and that they are empowered as readers, leading them naturally into the critical reading in the next lesson.

Learning objectives

- To investigate how characters are presented, referring to the text:

  ○ through dialogue, action and description;

  ○ how the reader responds to them;

  ○ through examining their relationships with other characters.

- To develop contributions to discussions about critical reading of the text.

Commentary

The learning objectives for this lesson clearly place the children as active readers who are able to investigate with integrity and make their own decisions about what the text is saying to them. It is significant in that it opens up a dialogue between young readers and allows for differences in opinion, as well as a consideration of what the writer intended. In this way, the learning fuses together reading responses and writer's craft in order to develop critical reading. Such depth and explicit managing of this type of reading will underpin the children's development as analytical readers as they move towards Key Stage 3. By setting up active and investigative reading the children are also moving forward as speakers and listeners as they learn to comprehend others' ideas and reactions.

Introduction to the lesson

After a recap about what was learnt at this point in the narrative you can move into some drama activities to support deeper learning and critical reading. To begin with, if the children have not done any work like this before, you will need to talk about how everyone is part of the drama which they will be undertaking and that there must be an atmosphere of trust and integrity. While some of the activities will seem as though someone else is doing the work, or only two people are standing up, all of the children are part of the drama of exploration into the fictional world. The real benefits for learning in this lesson and long term will only be realised if this is made clear, reiterated and adhered to.

Organise your room so that the children are sitting in a circle. Project Resource C on to the whiteboard and/or have a paper copy for the children. Read the extract to the children. Explain that they are now going to sculpt this part of the story; create a still image for them all to examine as a piece of three-dimensional text. Assuming that the above 'rules' and assumptions for the activity have been made clear, either ask for volunteers or choose two children to be Finn and Maia. This will depend upon the nature of the class, personalities in the room and how much drama work they have done in the past.

Resource C: page 100

Finn led her to the door of the hut. 'My father built it and we lived here whenever we weren't away on collecting trips. I still can't believe he isn't coming back, though it's four months since he was drowned.'

'Do you see him sometimes?' Maia asked – and he turned sharply because she seemed to have read his thoughts. 'I see mine. My father, not a ghost or an apparition … just him.'

'Yes. It's exactly like that. Often he's showing me something. A new insect or a plant.'

Now ask the two volunteers to stand in the middle of the circle and say that they are like the beginnings of a sculpture, the initial lump of clay; the rest of the class are going to do the hard work and sculpt Finn into the position they believe he will be in, when this conversation takes place. Then ask them to sculpt Maia into the scene according to their interpretation of the text. As children volunteer ideas, ensure that you are asking them why they think this and which part of the text led them to this interpretation. Threading the explicit commentary about how we read, learn and think critically will challenge them to think deeply and develop stamina for critical reading. As classes become more confident with this activity, getting individuals out of their seats to manoeuvre children will be part of the kinaesthetic process of manipulating their interpretation of the text. It should be stressed that the two children being sculpted are not contributing to the discussion and should be discouraged from doing so in order to keep the dimensions of the text and the readers.

Commentary

During this activity the children are visualising their thoughts and beginning to explore text, character and ideas in detail. They are offering an interpretation of text and justifying their ideas and developing their role as an active and critical reader. The sculpture may take on many forms during this process and once again the teacher can use this as an opportunity to talk about the fluidity of readers and differences of opinion. It also allows the teacher to plan for some higher order questions regarding empathy and relationships between characters at a time when children can access a three-dimensional version of the text. For example, how do you think Finn and Maia feel having just met each other? This will take on a different level of reading as the children are able to look at a 'live' version of this. Less able or reticent children can be invited to get out of their seat and have a look at the piece of text in greater detail, which often sparks a response to the text.

Once the children have had the opportunity to participate it is also a good time to model what you think at this point. The children will gain a great deal from hearing you speak alongside them as a reader as opposed to a teacher and you will be able to model language that conveys insight and critical thinking about something which began as a paragraph of black and white text.

Main lesson

Introduction

Now read the next extract to your class (Resource D, p102).

Resource D: page 102

'It looks fine. All of it.' She waved her hand over the hut, the boat, the lagoon. 'It looks like a place where one would want to stay for ever and ever.'

He gave her a startled glance. 'Yes, but I can't stay. I'm going on a journey.'

'Oh!' For a moment she was devastated. She had only just met him and now he was going away.

'I'm going to find the Xanti.'

This will completely change how the children have felt thus far about these two characters meeting. By delaying this part of the narrative, the teacher is in control of the process of reading and responding to fiction; something that most of us do at a high speed. By slowing down this process we are heightening the moments of empathy and emotional engagement with the text – the ideal opportunity to hone in on focused critical questioning of the children and making the reading process explicit to them.

Ask them how the sculpture might change. How will Finn and Maia's physical stance mirror any changes in their emotional demeanour? This is a complex question but with the right questioning from the teacher and direction to what they have already done, children will be able to make links between the extract, their reaction and the characters' reactions. The pulling together of these three things is scaffolding their learning and building their stamina for critical reading.

Next, ask the children if they can describe the space between Finn and Maia or the space around them. This activity is a way of measuring their understanding of the plot development and the relationship between characters. It is a simple activity to undertake but requires some deep thinking from the children. Have some strips of card and felt pens at hand to let them write down their words or phrases to describe the space (e.g. 'devastated', 'let down', 'disappointment'). They can then be asked to quietly get out of their seats and place the card where they believe they can see the emotion. By the end of this activity, even those children who may not have contributed will have heard model answers from their peers and there is a physical record of the responses intertwined with the three-dimensional text.

You can now use the communal voice activity to delve more deeply into this part of the text. Ask the children what the characters would say or think next? How would they change their voice and intonation if it was a thought or an audible comment? Can they convey this when they deliver their idea? What type of reading skill are they using here? These teacher questions will allow you to direct the activity into a meaningful critical response to the text. Once the children have had time to think or pair/share ideas and the room is settled, join the sculpture and model a thought for Finn or Maia. Stand behind the character you are speaking for and remain still and quiet, having told the class that you will do so until other volunteers join the sculpture and layer on their own thoughts and voices for Finn or Maia.

Ask a child to go and stand where they believe they are positioned as the reader. Ask other children if they agree with this positioning and get them to stand where they think the reader is positioned. Be open to different perspectives here and take care not to layer your own opinion at this point. This is an ideal opportunity to facilitate learning and allow the children's critical thinking to come to the fore. The lesson has been carefully scaffolded to this point in order to build confidence and stamina and children will feel ready to express a personal stance. Do ask them to qualify this, however, and having easy reference to the text itself will allow for links to be made. Question the children's justifications and unpick what criteria they are using. What does this tell us about individual interpretations on text?

As an additional challenge, you can now ask: *Can we place the reader and the writer? Can we describe the space between the reader and writer?* Asking individuals to place themselves can open up a deeper analytical conversation.

Commentary

The point at which a new piece of text changes our minds and therefore the sculpture, the children are consolidating previous critical readings of the text and learning that a reader's analysis can change. It is flexible to the movement within the narrative and our points of view move too; almost with the ebb and flow of the characters' experiences. The tension between Maia and Finn at this point in their conversation is different from a few moments ago, and so it leads us towards thinking about how the writer plans for our reactions through her craft and how we can manipulate others in our own writing.

When they are describing the space, the children are stepping outside the text and observing the three-dimensional version of the text objectively. This allows them to 'close read' a physical version of text and look for nuances of meaning that they may have missed at the first reading. They can flourish with experimental language without the fear of writing at this stage and begin to offer a critical reading. Doing this type of activity regularly can quickly build confidence and with effective, explicit teacher commentary will be more easily transferable as a skill to use with different types of text. Eventually, this will support children to be able to handle critical reading independently.

When we ask the children to contribute to a communal voice, they are still critically engaging with the text at this point but are also entering back into the narrative themselves and contributing to the wider connotations of this moment in the book. We can talk about how even advanced readers reflect on texts/stories in this way, either by wondering what a

(Continued)

(Continued)

character was thinking or what might happen next. It is helpful if the teacher offers some insight into her own experiences as a reader and continues to do so in reading lessons to layer this as a natural process for readers of all ages.

Finally, when the children are directed to place themselves as a reader or the writer these are opportunities to hone their critical analysis, still using a three-dimensional text as stimulus for close reading. At the same time, this activity is beginning to draw their focus away from just one aspect of the text or characters' interactions and prompting them to look at the bigger picture. Who else is in the scene? How is this meant to make us feel or react? Does it remind us of anything else?

Plenary

In pairs, ask the children to use mini whiteboards to note down what type of reading skills they think they used today. Ask them to explain to another pair what they have written. For example, skimming a text for clues when examining the sculpture, scanning the whole text for ideas when looking for ideas about the relationship between Finn and Maia, inferring how Maia might be feeling, predicting what will happen to her or Finn. Take some feedback from a few pairs who you have checked will be able to model this next level of reflective thinking well. With effective teacher commentary threading through the lesson and opportunity to reflect on the links between reading and the drama activities, this should be a natural next step for children.

Commentary

This plenary will allow you to bring all the different types of reading and analysis together and still retain a spirit of collaborative dialogue between peers. It is also the opportunity for you to measure how well your explicit management of the drama activities and the accompanying commentary has furthered the learnt experience for the children. There should be less feedback on the activities that they have 'done' and more about the reading and what they learnt when you listen in to the conversations around the room. What you learn at this point as the teacher will inform how you develop this type of analytical reading in the forthcoming lessons.

Assessment (measuring achievement)

Assessment for learning
- The degree of child participation, collaborative learning, focus on harnessing speaking and listening within drama are all excellent ways in which to formatively

assess the children in your class as they contribute or respond to these activities. It is important that this is not an ad hoc response and that you plan for the different learners in the class. It is worth considering to what extent you can plan for questions within the realms of analytical reading of texts and move the children towards more abstract concepts such as perspective. Careful planning in this area will give you greater confidence as a teacher managing these activities and more quickly build resilience and stamina in your young readers.

- Allowing space and time for reflection and peer assessment of contributions is another way in which you will be formatively assessing the children in your class. From their point of view, you are also slowing the process of critical reading for them and building a safe learning environment at the same time.

- Some readers will excel in this type of lesson and you will be able to ascertain where you will need to challenge them further in the next lesson; possibly through deeper questioning or offering alternative perspectives on the text for them to consider and respond to.

Assessment at the point of learning

- Make sure that you are prepared to manage the children's contributions during the lesson. How will you ensure that everyone has an opportunity to contribute to discussions? Will you use targeted questioning particularly using Bloom's taxonomy to help you to support or challenge different abilities of children? Will you use children who might normally dominate as the people to be sculpted in order to focus the dialogue and interactions on other children?

- Try to 'capture' good practice as it happens. Don't let it be subsumed into a bigger conversation. It might be that you stop the conversation to hone in on one of the contributions – *did you all hear that? What a thoughtful response. Could you repeat that for us? Thank you; let's try and work out why that is such a good analytical comment. Let's turn to our talk partner and have a minute to discuss that*. This allows you to manage the interactions with the children in your class in a meaningful and developmental way, as well as the children modelling good practice for their peers. It is also a lovely way to celebrate their deep thinking!

Assessment of learning

- After the lesson, you will have time to think about how the children involved themselves in the activities and how the plenary allowed you to fuse together all of the dialogue and learning which has taken place. Did the plenary capture what you thought had been learnt in the lesson? Were there any misconceptions of reading concepts or of the narrative itself which you will need to follow up? How will this lead you to plan for the next lesson and moving forward with the narrative? Would similar activities be useful to consolidate learning or is your class ready to deal with some text independently and offer some critical comment on it?

- In this type of lesson, have all the children had the opportunity to be involved or to learn from the involvement of others? How will you manage this next time? Did it become apparent in the plenary that your explicit teacher commentary had supported all children in learning more about themselves as critical readers and how to approach a text in order to delve more deeply? Perhaps a short response from children in the next lesson on what the writer was thinking would be a way in which you could measure their understanding of writer's craft and perspective.

Challenges

- Some children may be reticent with drama activities and some may associate the idea with having to perform in front of an audience. The type of activities described above will allow the teacher to reiterate the idea that all children are part of the drama, but that this may not mean standing up in front of the class and that contributions will be through a scaffolded and layered discussion. There is the opportunity to build confidence and enjoyment of building the drama together and ensure that this is done collaboratively. Likewise, this will depend on the teacher's insistence on keeping the dramatic atmosphere within the room, listening to each other and adding layers of meaning thoughtfully. The use of music can often help here.

- Another challenge might be children who are very confident and could possibly dominate the class discussions. On these occasions, paired discussions first and using directed questioning will help. For sculpted activities, you might choose a child who has previously contributed a lot to discussions, to be the 'clay' in the centre of the circle. This will allow other children to have time to think and come forward with their ideas.

- As ever, planning teacher questions in advance will support you with managing these aspects of the lessons. The opportunity to target individuals to develop a reading skill further can be fulfilled through using a structure such as Bloom's taxonomy (Bloom, 1956 – see Figures 3.2 and 3.3 in Chapter 3) to ensure that time is used efficiently to allow for focused formative assessment.

Application of learning

Links to other areas of the curriculum

Exploring texts through drama is powerful and valid in other areas of the curriculum, particularly when undertaking topic-based approaches that will enable the linking and connection of ideas. It would also be a way of promoting the exploration of different viewpoints if using a range of source materials to support a fiction text.

Next lesson

Following on from this, it will be interesting to ascertain the children's predictions regarding the identity of Miss Minton and why Finn might be questioning Maia about Miss Minton's full name (p107).

Chapter 8 takes us back to the story from Clovis' viewpoint as he has escaped the theatre company to find the Carters' house. Can the children predict his reception? Exploring the reactions of the twins and Clovis and Maia's feelings could be explored through further drama work leading into a creative written response.

Learning outcomes review

You should now have knowledge and understanding of how the use of drama strategies can not only engage children in their learning but also be used to explicitly develop critical reading of texts. You should be able to make links between the way in which this text was handled and how you might approach other texts similarly. You should have learnt how to thread the explicit learning commentary through the lesson, sharing the learning direction with the children to ensure that they are better able to reflect on what they have done and what skills they have developed.

This lesson and further ideas are just one way in which some of these strategies can be used. It might lead you to consider how the sense of progression is handled between key stages so that children are learning to be actively involved in text from an early age and encouraged to become part of a living, three-dimensional text, affording them greater opportunity for critical insight.

Further reading

Bunyan, P and Moore, R (2005) *NATE Drama Packs Introductory Pack: Drama within English 11–16*. Sheffield: NATE.

Published by the National Association for the Teaching of English (NATE), these materials are well worth visiting for creative ideas on how to use some of the strategies described here and many others. Each scheme of work is accompanied by a teacher commentary, which is useful when approaching this for the first time and all strategies are easily adaptable to Key Stage 1 and Key Stage 2.

Cremin, T (2009) *Teaching English Creatively*. London: Taylor and Francis Ltd.

A useful book exploring what it means to teach creatively in primary schools. It explores how we can engage children with reading and writing and offers a range of insights and ideas.

References

Alexander, R (2004) *Towards Dialogic Teaching: Rethinking Classroom Talk*. York: Dialogos UK.

Beattie, L and Highfield, N (2007) Creating curious readers through drama: drama and textual exploration. *English Drama Media*, 8: 27–9.

Bloom, BS (1956) *Taxonomy of Educational Objectives: The Classification of Educational Goals, by a Committee of College and University Examiners. Handbook I: Cognitive Domain.* New York: Longmans, Green.

Department for Education (DfE) (2013) *The National Curriculum in England: Framework Document.* London: DfE.

Franks, A (2015) Talk and drama: seeing voices, in Brindley, S and Marshall, B (eds.) *Master Class in English Education.* London: Bloomsbury, pp141–56.

Hall, C (2015) Understanding reading, in Brindley, S and Marshall, B (eds.) *Master Class in English Education.* London: Bloomsbury, pp61–71.

Ibbotson, E (2002) *Journey to the River Sea.* London: Macmillan Children's Books.

Ketch, A (2005) Conversation: the comprehension connection. *The Reader Teacher*, 59 (1): 8–13.

McGuinn, N (2014) *The English Teacher's Drama Handbook.* London: Routledge.

Mercer, N (2000) *Words and Minds: How We Use Language to Think Together.* London: Routledge.

Neelands, J (1984) *Making Sense of Drama.* Oxford: Heinemann Educational Books.

Pressley, M (2000) What should comprehension instruction be the instruction of? in Kamil, ML, Mosenthal, PB, Pearson, PD and Barr, R (eds.) *Handbook of Reading Research: Volume III.* New York: Lawrence Erlbaum.

Rojos-Drummond, S and Mercer, N (2003) Scaffolding the development of effective collaboration and learning. *International Journal of Education Research*, 39: 99–111.

Chapter 10

Year 5: Using moving image to develop critical reading

Learning outcomes

This chapter explores how children respond to moving image and how teachers can use it to develop critical reading.

This chapter will allow you to achieve the following outcomes:

- build upon children's understanding of texts, including visual and multimodal forms;
- develop strategies for handling moving image to extend thinking;
- understand how to plan for critical reading of short films.

Teachers' Standards

Working through this chapter will help you meet the following standards:

2. Promote good progress and outcomes by pupils.
3. Demonstrate good subject and curriculum knowledge.
4. Plan and teach well-structured lessons.
6. Make accurate and productive use of assessment.

Links to the National Curriculum

Years 5 and 6 programme of study

READING – Comprehension
Pupils should be taught to:

- maintain positive attitudes to reading and understanding what they read by:

  ✓ continuing to read and discuss an increasingly wide range of fiction, poetry, plays, non-fiction and reference books or textbooks
  ✓ reading books that are structured in different ways and reading for a range of purposes

- ✓ increasing their familiarity with a wide range of books, including myths, legends, and traditional stories, modern fiction, fiction from our literary heritage, and books from their cultures and traditions
- ✓ recommending books that they have read to their peers, giving reasons for their choices
- ✓ identifying and discussing themes and conventions in and across a wide range of writing
- ✓ making comparisons within and across books
- ✓ learning a wider range of poetry by heart
- ✓ preparing poems and plays to read aloud and to perform, showing understanding through intonation, tone and volume so that the meaning is clear to an audience

- understand what they read by:

  - ✓ checking that the book makes sense to them, discussing their understanding and exploring the meaning of words in context
  - ✓ asking questions to improve their understanding
  - ✓ drawing inferences such as inferring characters' feelings, thoughts and motives from their actions, and justifying inferences with evidence
  - ✓ predicting what might happen from details stated and implied
  - ✓ summarising the main ideas drawn from more than one paragraph, identifying key details that support the main ideas
  - ✓ identifying how language, structure and presentation contribute to meaning

- discuss and evaluate how authors use language, including figurative language, considering the impact on the reader
- distinguish between statements of fact and opinion
- retrieve, record and present information from non-fiction
- participate in discussions about books that are read to them and those they can read for themselves, building on their own and others' ideas and challenging views courteously
- explain and discuss their understanding of what they have read, including through formal presentations and debates, maintaining a focus on the topic and using notes where necessary
- provide reasoned justifications for their views.

(DfE, 2013)

Key focus: Developing reading comprehension through the appreciation of film

Activity

Think about the last film you watched. What was it that drew you to the film? Is it a genre that you would normally read in traditional text form? Did this work differently in your reaction to it in the film mode? Was it a sociable experience? Did you discuss it with your friends, family or colleagues? To what extent did these conversations delve deeply into theme, characterisation or plot development? Did you begin to co-construct meaning?

Sometimes we underestimate the powerful nature of films in stimulating the same cognitive processes and reading comprehension as more traditional texts. Not only is it an exciting means of collaborative learning and appreciation of media, but it is also a way in which we can reflect on the reading process and how to develop these skills further.

Maine (2013) describes reading as *the act of making meaning from text, in whatever its form, whether written, visual or multimodal* (Maine, 2013, p151). In developing an awareness and analytical understanding of visual literacy, we necessarily develop the area of reading to include moving image. Reid (2015) goes on to describe literacy as *being able to fully participate in a culture* (Reid, 2015, p84). Within this pedagogical realm, the value and significance of media education is not to be underestimated. As well as a child's entitlement to enjoy and understand media in all of its forms, Reid goes on to explore a *social, participatory model of literacy*, of which film is an important part (Reid, 2015, p89)

We have considered up to this point how children need to be able to understand the language associated with a text if they are truly to comprehend it. The same is true of film language and this consideration needs to be taken into account when looking at long-term planning for our children. Where does film literacy fit into our teaching? What are the significant learning factors we would want to consider? What foundations are we building for film literacy at Key Stage 3 and the children's understanding of the culture around them? How do we develop film language?

In building a curriculum that looks at creating meaning through reading, we are contributing to a wider definition of literacy and one that will inevitably include a range of texts beyond a traditional canon. We have moved through looking at reading from the early years into Key Stage 2, developing young readers' minds to view meanings as fluid and ever changing with different contexts and perspectives. We have asked them to draw on prior experiences, ask questions, conjure up images and make predictions (Pressley, 2006). There is, in all of this, a natural moment when our view of what constitutes a 'text' in all of its glorious forms needs to be shared and communicated to children.

Examining and talking about film fosters exploratory talk. In its very essence, a conversation about film may become a tentative review, allowing for hypothetical questions and encouraging of a peer's differing opinion (Barnes and Todd, 1995). It would seem that the benefits of exploring film to develop an extension of 'literacy' and to ensure a cultural identity within the world would necessitate our consideration of where this features in our teaching.

Choosing a film text can be enjoyable in its own right, particularly with the support of some very helpful education websites (see further reading below). As with a traditional text, the key will be one that will engage our learners, is open to interpretation and encourages a degree of negotiation when exploring meaning. A well-chosen film text will incite imagination and empathy to contribute to an investment in the text and the teacher can plan to facilitate dialogic talk during exploratory activities. In the example below, the introduction is grounded in a concrete experience and possible emotion to focus children on empathy and understanding of characters' predicaments.

As well as developing key reading skills, the joint exploration of a film text will facilitate the co-construction of meaning and ways to support the children in managing their own reactions in order to create a critical response to their peers' ideas. In addition, it draws on the scaffolding and framing of questions explored in Chapter 9.

Teaching your class: Year 5

The lesson outlined here gives some ideas on how to plan for using film texts to further develop inference and deduction leading to analytical thinking. There is a wide range of short films available to use as media texts in this way. Suggested strategies will engage the children in digital texts with all the accompanying nuances of meaning. I have chosen here to use a short film called *Replay* (The Literacy Shed, **www.literacyshed. com/the-inspiration-shed.html**). There is limited amount of dialogue in it and it is in French so you can choose to focus on this or not. There are versions with sub-titles. The music is also worthy of exploration and can often be a creative way into a media text.

Context

This film can potentially be used as part of a media scheme of work, where the children have been exploring moving images. Alternatively, it may be linked by theme to a fiction text that has been read as a class. The theme of the narrative is about a post-apocalyptic world and a surviving girl and her younger brother. It might be linked to a text by this theme or the theme of family relationships, surviving turbulent times or the lure of another world.

To give an emotional context, ask the children to discuss in groups when they last had an argument or disagreement with someone they love/like. This might be a family member or a close friend. This will allow for some ownership as the dialogue ensues, with a clear context for the children. Ask for some examples from the room and ask how these situations were resolved. The children can now write down some vocabulary for how they felt during the disagreement and how they felt afterwards. Collect four or five examples from the class and record them on the whiteboard. Ask the children if they can help you to put them into an order for a 'shades of meaning' exercise. Are some words stronger than others? Does that matter? Why might some people have used such strong words?

To extend this vocabulary work, these questions will challenge the children to reflect on their choices and be critical about them. Would they change any words? Do their choices link to context? So, why is context important? This structured activity will allow them to build towards a more conceptual reading of context and consider the power of language.

Learning objectives

- To analyse how we are led to empathise with the main characters.

- To make inferences based on what we see happening in the film.

- To participate in discussions about making meaning through moving images.

Commentary

The work prior to this lesson will allow the teacher to contextualise the idea of empathy based on children's discussions. A reminder about skimming and scanning to look for overall understanding and smaller clues in texts will be supportive of the learning objective to make inferences based on what we see happening in the film. *Depending on the amount of film work the children have done previously, it will be worth spending some time on how reading skills are still applicable to moving image and, in fact, can support and develop them, i.e. inference and deduction. It is an ideal opportunity to talk about how often the children display good reading skills when they are watching TV, at the cinema, looking at adverts or playing interactive computer games.*

Introduction to the lesson

Play the first minute of the film without showing the children the visuals (1 minute 10 seconds from the first title). Provide them with a sheet to collect ideas (an A4 sheet, quartered into story, character, time and place) if they wish to jot down notes during the audio extract. Ask them what they imagine might be happening. If this is their first introduction to the post-apocalyptic theme, then responses may be varied.

Depending on the children's ability, some tables might require vocabulary prompts or a teaching assistant to support them. Reassure them that they do not have to write lots of words down; just a few initial responses as they thought of them. Some boxes might be left blank.

Allow them to have time on tables to share their ideas and move around the room to ascertain different types of interpretations. When they have had a few minutes to discuss this, ask for some feedback. Again, depending on where this sits within a scheme, some children might be making links to themes you have discovered in your reading of a class text.

Commentary

The use of short film with key 'reading' activities can build reading stamina and offer an alternative way of building these skills. With regular reflection and commentary on these types of activities it can build confidence and increase the children's own awareness of their capabilities.

By allowing the children to hear the introduction to the film before they see it, we are suggesting to them that, like other texts, this is open to different interpretations. It does not matter if some of their suggestions on plot or character mirror what is actually in the film. We are allowing them to connect, creatively and emotionally, to diagetic and non-diagetic sounds. They will hear footsteps, laboured breathing, a door banging (diagetic sounds) and a short sequence of music (non-diagetic sounds). Therefore, they will have real life prompts to respond to and a more artistic perspective on the narrative which may lead them to consider more creative or mood driven responses.

Some children may not want to write during the playing of the audio. Not all children will think in a linear fashion about what they hear and what they think might be happening. Some will want to hear the minute of audio and then consider the extract as a 'whole' and respond in that way. You should plan accordingly for this and make sure that this is explained in your initial instructions.

Main lesson

Introduction

Now play the film to the children. They will need time to process what they have seen and an opportunity to talk at the end of the film will be beneficial. Tables should have some prompt questions on A3 paper to structure their talk; how did this make you feel? Did you relate to the sister or the brother? Could you see both of their points of view? Was it a happy or sad ending? Can you explain why you think this?

Giving the children time to talk around the questions will not only give them a focus but also enable you to take feedback which is based on empathy, an understanding of character, an awareness of a problem with two different viewpoints, mood and the beginnings of analysis. Note that the planning of the questions enables us to layer the type of critical reading we would like the children to undertake and prepares them cognitively for an analytical approach. It is worth recording some responses on flipchart paper and saying explicitly that they have had a first reading of the film and these are their first reactions to the text. A reader will make judgements about a story and the characters very quickly; sometimes we miss extra clues that the writer/director has given us and a second 'reading' will allow us to delve into the text in more depth.

There are a number of ways to focus on this text and this will need to be planned in advance or continue into a sequence of lessons. A close reading of the text will allow the teacher to focus on film language. In this instance, I think the following are worthy of further exploration and will allow children to build on their inference and deduction skills. This would also allow for six groups to work on different aspects.

1. Setting and costume (limited range of colours, hostile outside environment, bare looking interior in the 'home').

2. Lighting (low key lighting to reflect apocalyptic world, a metaphor for the sense of loss of community and brightness which comes from a range of relationships).

3. Camera movement (worth showing extract where Lana is looking for Theo and where he is looking around the playground to compare the new and old worlds).

4. Camera framing (some significant moments with the zooming in towards the tape recorder, the focus on the two mugs).

5. Sound (diagetic, non-diagetic, use of music, silence).

6. Dialogue (why is it only used in the first part of the film? What does it represent and how does it convey mood?).

For this activity, groups can be given a different focus. Ideally, where there is the technological capacity, it would be best for the children to re-watch the film on a laptop/tablet in groups and pause at moments in the 'text' that they want to focus on, to do some close reading. They can be given a note-taking sheet to fill in as they respond. You will want to give a clear time target and expected outcome at this point, and this will be gauged by the ability level of the class and table groupings.

Commentary

The planned learning allows time to have group discussions about meaning, promoting collaborative approaches to learning and reiterating how the reader makes sense of text. It links back to years of reading comprehension and now links understanding of authorial intent to that of another text maker: a film director. The discussions during the lesson should allow for meaning to be layered through collaborative work and increase awareness of their own constructed understanding.

Plenary

As a plenary it would be useful to get groups to swap with another group to read about their responses to a different focus. They can move to the laptop/tablet when the film has been paused at a suitable point, watch a short part of the film and look at the notes that have been made. If they have anything to add or have a different perspective, they should write this in a different colour. Groups then return to their original place and review any comments.

As a teacher, you should stress that meaning can be multi-layered or come from a different perspective – a skill which they are developing today and will support them in being more confident critical readers. You could ask one of the more able children if they are able to link this reading skill to some reading they have done with the class reader or in another subject area.

Commentary

The conversations you have heard on tables and the type of responses to peers' work will give you an insight into the next steps in learning. Many classes will need the beginning of the next lesson to review their reading of the text and to revisit the film. How all of this is used to maximise learning is outlined in the next lesson section.

Assessment (measuring achievement)

Assessment for learning
- Utilising the explicit teacher commentary alongside the focused learning objectives is an excellent way to gauge the children's understanding of reading skills used with moving images as well as setting the scene for today's learning.

- The plenary is an effective way of using peer review to capture what learning has taken place. It moves the children laterally to another cognitive approach and gives them some ownership of the assessment process through peers. All of this is ongoing work and simply feeds into the next lesson, so should be reassuring for children, especially getting feedback as a group as opposed to individually.

Assessment at the point of learning

- The nature of the group work allows the teacher to 'eavesdrop' on conversations to ascertain engagement, understanding and focus. Where intervention is needed at this point, it is appropriate to give it, but where groups are involved in solid, exploratory talk the teacher should resist getting involved in the process at this stage. The plenary will give more information as regards planning for the next lesson.

Assessment of learning

- Reflection on the lesson and taking in the groups' written responses to their close reading will give you some understanding of their critical engagement with the texts. Where some groups are not delving as deeply into the text, ask yourself why this might be; consider the group make-up, the area of focus itself; was it too complex an idea? Was it the genre? Your thoughts on this will be significant in helping you to plan the next stage of learning.

Challenges

- Thinking about the grouping of children is important in terms of how they work collaboratively, matching ability to task/focus and considering behaviours. Likewise, the movement of children around the room to look at another group's work will require careful instructions.

- Some children may need additional prompts when first getting into their groups with a reading focus. In this instance, planning some prompt questions in advance as an additional resource will be useful in ensuring that they can start the task quickly without becoming disengaged.

Application of learning

Links to other areas of the curriculum

The nature of this film will inevitably link to aspects of personal, social and health education. The themes of sibling tension and bereavement are ones that might be particularly sensitive or relevant to a class and therefore thinking about the handling of this film is important.

Next lesson

Following on from today's learning, the next lesson should give the children the opportunity to hear from the different groups and have some input on different aspects of film language. It would be interesting to build on collaborative learning at this point by using a variation of the envoy and jigsaw strategy. The groups should number themselves 1–6 and ensure that one person then goes to each table to gather information on the area of reading focus. The person left on the table is the expert who explains their critical response to the newcomers. Everyone returns to their original table and adds to a sheet with the six areas of focus clearly labelled on it. This will allow for more efficient feeding back of ideas and ensures that children will have had the experience of some close reading and a holistic consideration of the text.

It would be useful to allow the children to write about their responses to the film from a reader's point of view, commenting on how the director's craft led them to their interpretation. This would facilitate the use of meaningful film language and show the children the extent of their critical reading skills. Depending on the class, there will be different expectations in terms of depth and some scaffold structures might be useful.

It goes without saying that using this film as a springboard into creative writing is an obvious next step and children can imagine what happened next and write another ending.

Learning outcomes review

Following on from previous chapters on visual literacy, you should now be able to see the links between using still images or picture books and moving images. The lesson should have emphasised the power of short films in the literacy classroom, both in developing greater critical reading and providing an excellent springboard into creative writing. The explicit commentary is, once again, at the heart of all planned strategies, to ensure that the learning is realised as part of a process for the children and that they are able to transfer this learning to other texts – both written and image based.

Further reading

English and Media Centre (2008) *English Allsorts*. London: Stephens and George Ltd.

This is a useful and practical text to support teachers with ideas for the teaching of media. Each page suggests an age range, duration of time and a list of activities. The book is organised into sections such as speaking and listening, reading any text, poetry, etc., but also has an alternative index to group lesson ideas differently.

www.literacyshed.com – a fantastic website with lots of ideas for the busy teacher who enjoys using new and creative ways to engage children with visual literacy.

www.filmeducation.org – a useful website for film resources and teaching support.

www.bfi.org.uk – the British Film Institute's website with archives and lots of resources to support teachers.

References

Barnes, D and Todd, F (1995) *Communication and Learning Revisited: Making Meaning Through Talk.* Portsmouth, NH: Boynton Cook.

Department for Education (DfE) (2013) *The National Curriculum in England: Framework Document.* London: DfE.

Literacy Shed, The. Available at: **www.literacyshed.com/the-inspiration-shed.html**

Maine, F (2013) How children talk together to make meaning from texts: a dialogic perspective on reading comprehension strategies. *Literacy*, 47 (3): 150–6.

Pressley, M (2006) *Reading Instruction that Works: The Case for Balanced Teaching* (3rd edn.). London: Guilford Press.

Reid, M (2015) Film, literacy and cultural participation, in Brindley, S and Marshall, B (eds.) *Master Class in English Education*. London: Bloomsbury, pp84–96.

Smith, V (2010) Comprehension is a social act, in Hall, K, Goswami, U, Harrison, C, Ellis, S and Soler, J (eds.) *Interdisciplinary Perspectives on Learning to Read: Culture, Cognition and Pedagogy*. London: Routledge, pp61–73.

Chapter 11

Year 6: Using drama to analyse a Shakespeare text

Teachers' Standards

Working through this chapter will help you meet the following standards:

1. Set high expectations which inspire, motivate and challenge pupils.
2. Promote good progress and outcomes by pupils.
3. Demonstrate good subject and curriculum knowledge.
4. Plan and teach well-structured lessons.
5. Adapt teaching to respond to the strengths and needs of all pupils.

Links to the National Curriculum

Years 5 and 6 programme of study

READING – Comprehension
Pupils should be taught to:

- maintain positive attitudes to reading and understanding what they read by:

- ✓ continuing to read and discuss an increasingly wide range of fiction, poetry, plays, non-fiction and reference books or textbooks
- ✓ increasing their familiarity with a wide range of books, including myths, legends, and traditional stories, modern fiction, fiction from our literary heritage, and books from their cultures and traditions
- ✓ identifying and discussing themes and conventions in and across a wide range of writing
- ✓ making comparisons within and across books
- ✓ preparing poems and plays to read aloud and to perform, showing understanding through intonation, tone and volume so that the meaning is clear to an audience

- understand what they read by:

  - ✓ checking that the book makes sense to them, discussing their understanding and exploring the meaning of words in context
  - ✓ asking questions to improve their understanding
  - ✓ drawing inferences such as inferring characters' feelings, thoughts and motives from their actions, and justifying inferences with evidence
  - ✓ predicting what might happen from details stated and implied
  - ✓ summarising the main ideas drawn from more than one paragraph, identifying key details that support the main ideas
  - ✓ identifying how language, structure and presentation contribute to meaning

- discuss and evaluate how authors use language, including figurative language, considering the impact on the reader
- participate in discussions about books that are read to them and those they can read for themselves, building on their own and others' ideas and challenging views courteously
- explain and discuss their understanding of what they have read
- provide reasoned justifications for their views.

(DfE, 2013)

Key focus: Reading comprehension of challenging texts

Activity

Let us consider your first experience of Shakespeare. Was it at primary or secondary school? Was it an enjoyable experience? Think through your response to this last question and consider what contributed to this. Can you remember your first experience of seeing Shakespeare performed, either on the stage or on film?

Thinking through your own experiences should enable you to reflect on what is special about studying a Shakespearean play. How can you accumulate all of your understanding of reading comprehension, active approaches to reading and collaborative learning to create your own philosophy on teaching Shakespeare? What will engage and excite the children in your class? How will you ensure that they enjoy the experience?

Exploring and enjoying Shakespeare at an early age can be a delight and the beginning of a whole new experience. Equally, for many teachers, it can offer some anxiety and challenges in terms of how to approach difficult texts with children. Keeping the drama at the heart of what we plan can be the first step towards managing these tensions and ensuring that the children not only enjoy their experiences but also develop as readers and thinkers.

As Gibson (1998) suggests, *a powerful argument for studying Shakespeare exists in his extraordinariness, his strangeness, his unfamiliarity. His appeal lies in a unique blend of the unfamiliar and the strange, his relevance and his remoteness* (Gibson, 1998, p6). Active approaches to the text will enable the children to explore, hypothesise, predict, argue, empathise and share the experience of challenging ideas and language within the sphere of some familiar concepts: relationships, love, hate and rivalry to name but a few (Gibson, 1998).

The focus of the lesson can be on themes, character and motivation, language or the complexities of the plot itself. It is the way in which we plan to expose these literary concepts to the children that will be at the heart of any positive outcome. The strengths in collaborative learning and how we encourage children to talk about their thoughts in response to these concepts will be developing not only their critical reading, but also their ability to express opinions and justify a stance. Equally, the shared experiences can lead to other imaginative and creative journeys. In so doing, the children will also be developing their understanding of people and the world we live in (Boyd, 2010).

Thinking about the engagement of the children in initial 'reading' of the text will be the point at which they make the first level of inference, usually creating a literal understanding of the text. The active strategies described below will allow the opportunity to explore more deeply and make controlled inferences based on reflection and collaboration (Tennent, 2015). It is this layered approach to reading and making meaning which will give the children a sense of satisfaction and confidence while leading them towards a more critical understanding of the text – all within the realms of collaboration and creativity.

Introducing the text in small, accessible segments can also be significant in building confidence with the children. Allowing them to hear it read aloud to convey meaning (modelling the language for them) and planning time for them to experiment with it themselves will begin to remove perceptions of the language as a barrier. Saying lines aloud in a safe environment will enable the children to become attuned to the language and therefore more able to make sense of the text with their peers (Yandell and Franks, 2014).

Teaching your class: Year 6

The lesson described below gives a practical approach for exploring a Shakespearean text with Year 6. The focus is on having an understanding of the importance of theme, mood and atmosphere and how these contribute to the dramatic tension in the play. Many of the activities are easily adaptable for other plays and texts, but I have chosen here to look at *The Tempest*. This text has many layers of meaning and can be studied at Key Stage 4, 5 or beyond. However, there are many themes that will also lend themselves to the engagement of younger children who are interested in sibling rivalry, revenge, the supernatural, good versus evil and forgiveness. The earlier scenes are an excellent way to explore pathetic fallacy and how this contributes to mood and other thematic approaches.

Context

The children will have explored the opening scenes of Act 1 and focused on the shipwreck. Act 1 Scene 1 is full of the action of the storm at sea and lends itself to using segments of text to make sense of the action and consider what atmosphere introduces us to the play. Some well-chosen extracts (see some examples below) will enable groups of children to adopt an investigative approach to the text to find clues for what is happening. They can all have the same clues on pieces of card and decide on a group understanding and representation of this. This approach of an open mind and willingness to explore collaboratively will support them in feeling confident when looking at unusual language. Likewise, the active learning will mean that they are engaged interactively with the text as well as being challenged mentally to deal with different ideas to arrive at a final 'picture'. Their interpretation might be shown through a mind map with images to support it or a freeze frame with a caption on card. They should have been given clear instructions on how long they have to do this and given some prompt questions to scaffold their group discussions: Who is in this scene? What is happening? Is everyone working together? What do you predict will happen? How will this action move on if this is the opening to a play?

A plenary which draws out how they decided on their freeze frame or mind map will promote the evaluation of their critical reading, thus cementing their collaborative learning and a recognition that there may be other interpretations of the same text.

Suitable segments of text to explore in Act 1 Scene 1

- *[On a ship at sea]: a tempestuous noise of thunder and lightning heard.*
- *Enter mariners.*
- Take in the topsail. Tend to th' master's whistle.
- *A cry within.* A plague upon this howling! They are louder than the weather or our office.
- Have you a mind to sink?
- … though the ship were no stronger than a nutshell …
- All lost, to prayers, to prayers! all lost!
- *A confused noise within:* "Mercy on us!"
- Let's all sink wi' th' King.

Learning objectives

- To deduce meaning from Shakespearean language.

- To make inferences based on what is happening in the plot.

- To explore interpretations of text and arrive at a personal understanding.

Commentary

These objectives should make clear to the children that they are building on previous understanding of inferring and deducing within a text. The skills that they have acquired and developed over the key stage are being put to good use by exploring a different type of language within a new genre of text, the play. The opportunity to explore different meanings with peers allows for an open and exciting approach to Shakespeare. Will our initial predictions follow through? Will we change our minds about characters or what else might happen? Can we imagine some of the scenes by being out of our seats and exploring parts of the text for ourselves?

To extend their understanding of the context of the storm within the plot, Act 1 Scene 2, Lines 193–206 is a useful extract to follow on with. Here, we hear a report of the storm from the spirit, Ariel, who summoned up a storm to follow his master's orders. When looking at the rest of this scene, it could lead into an exploration of these two characters and how the theme of power and authority runs through the play.

Introduction to the lesson

Having introduced the theme of magic through looking at Prospero's conjuring up of the storm with the help of the spirit, Ariel, the children can free themselves up for some prediction activities without being bound by the realms of common sense and logic. The plot has elements of the unknown and the supernatural, which is the perfect theme to use as a springboard into creative ideas about what might happen next. Some plot developments and 'back story' will need to have been shared by this point to ensure that the children are aware of the ill-feeling that Prospero has for Antonio, who usurped his place as the Duke of Milan. Discussing how this would make us feel, particularly if a family member had treated us this way, will be useful in laying some foundations for these predictions.

You may choose to put the children into groups with a key question to consider together. The act of collaborating about this, hypothesising and speculating about characters' reactions or actions, will engage the children with their ideas. There may be some disagreements and the children can be encouraged to explain their viewpoint and defend their prediction to their peers. If there are tablets or flip cameras available, it would be useful for them to record their predictions at this point.

Questions to prompt groups for their predictions could include the following:

- What will Prospero do or say to his brother Antonio and King Alonso?
- What might happen when Miranda and Ferdinand meet on the island?
- Who else might be on the ship who is important to the story of Prospero?
- What might Caliban do if he meets strangers on the island?

Commentary

The exploratory talk that takes place here should be the culmination of effective group work over a number of years. The sense of progression that runs through this book is indicative of the long-term planning and year on year consolidation of reading skills. The regular use of speaking and listening, used both as a tool and as a significant part of learning in its own right, will ensure that children in Year 6 are fully participative in exploratory talk. As researched by Alexander (2004), there is great value in planning for collaboration and peer group discussions throughout their learning journey. At this stage, your class of children should be confident within the supportive learning environment and enjoy sharing and exploring ideas in response to literary texts, safe in the knowledge that they have a right to an interpretation and prediction too.

Main lesson

Introduction

At this point the children should be sitting in a circle with no desks. Based on some of the drama techniques used in the previous chapter, they should be aware that they are going to explore some of their predictions through drama. You will need a volunteer to play the parts of Prospero, Ferdinand, Miranda and Ariel.

Explain to the children that Ariel evokes more magic – but this time for Ferdinand, son to the King of Naples. Ariel sings a song convincing Ferdinand that his father has drowned at sea. As Prospero and Miranda listen, they hear Ferdinand commenting on the music:

Act 1 Scene 2, Lines 408–410

The ditty does remember my drown'd father.

This is no mortal business, nor no sound

That the earth owes: – I hear it now above me.

This will be the cue, with some well-chosen music, for the children to begin their exploration of what happens next. The four characters in the scene can be placed in the middle of the circle and positioned where the children think would best suit this point in the plot.

Ask the groups who were predicting what would happen when Ferdinand and Miranda met about their ideas. Ask the rest of the class if this would change the positions that the characters are standing in. Have some strips of card ready with segments of text either printed or written in a large font. Working flexibly with the predictions that you receive from the class, add in a new segment of text for the class to consider (examples on the following page). Depending on the ability level of the children, you may want them to have some paired discussion for one or two minutes to think through some initial reactions. It would also be helpful to have the segments of text projected on to the white board.

There will be a layering of text presented to the children which will ask them to (a) deal with the challenges of some possibly unfamiliar language, (b) consider the development of plot and changing relationship between characters, and (c) consider why Shakespeare crafted the plot this way. You will want to plan in advance what questions you might challenge more able children with in order to develop their critical thinking further.

Segments of text to explore in Act 1 Scene 2, Lines 408–504:

– *Miranda*: What is 't? a spirit? (412)
– *Prospero*: No, wench; it eats and sleeps and hath such senses

---

132

As we have, such. (415–16)

– *Miranda*: I might call him a thing divine. (420)

– *Ferdinand*: Most sure the goddess
On whom these airs attend! (424–25)

– *Ferdinand*: I weep: myself am Naples …
The King my father wrack'd. (437–39)

– *Prospero*: [aside] At the first sight
They have chang'd eyes. Delicate Ariel,
I'll set thee free for this. (443–45)

– *Prospero*: They are both in either's pow'rs: but this
swift business
I must uneasy make, lest too light winning
Make the prize light. (453–55)

– *Prospero (to Miranda)*: Follow me.
Speak not you for him: he's a traitor. Come. (462–63)

– *Miranda*: O dear father,
Make not too rash a trial of him, for
He's gentle, and not fearful. (469–471)

– *Prospero (to Miranda)*: Thou think'st there are no more such shapes as he,
Having seen but him and Caliban: foolish wench! (481–82)

– *Miranda (to Ferdinand)*: Be of comfort;
My father's of a better nature, sir,
Than he appears by speech. (498–500)

– *Prospero (Ariel)*: Thou shalt be as free
As mountain winds: but then exactly do
All points of my command. (501–03)

– *Ariel*: To th' syllable. (503)

Commentary

These drama strategies allow the teacher to manage a class discussion which focuses on an 'image' in the middle of the room. The children in the outer circle take control of the image or sculpture and it will be something for them to consider in a concrete fashion while dealing with extracts from the scene. As with the activities described in Chapter 9, it allows the children to be part of the drama but not necessarily in the spotlight.

By introducing text slowly, you will be managing their confidence levels and guiding them towards having a positive experience of reading a Shakespearean text critically. The segments

(Continued)

(Continued)

suggested are for guidance and your own reading or focus for the scene might require some additions or different lines. You will need to consider how you manage introducing them to the sculpture in the centre and what types of questions you will ask to support the children. Remember to talk explicitly about their investigative skills – inference and deduction – and that you are keen to hear how they respond and make a decision about the plot development. They might do some pair/share talk before offering ideas to the bigger reading of the text in the centre of the room. This approach opens up a range of interpretations and, as well as being fun for the children, is challenging them to undertake some critical reading.

Plenary

Using some of the recorded predictions regarding what would happen if Miranda and Ferdinand met, play these to the class. Ask them to revisit these predictions in light of what they have discovered now. Is this what they expected? Did the four characters in this part of the scene behave as they thought they would?

Anticipate moving the plot forward next lesson and ask them where they think the other passengers from the ship have gone. How will this impact on Prospero, Miranda and Ferdinand differently?

Commentary

This plenary will revisit predictions and require children to reflect on their previous thinking. All of this is challenging initial responses to text and asking them to think specifically about their critical reading skills. In recognising that there may be different predictions, we are supporting them in their growing awareness that there can be a range of interpretations. The second part of the plenary links this thinking to the next part of the plot and therefore encourages the children to connect the 'activities' to a process of reading that they are moving through in order to make sense of the text as a whole.

Assessment (measuring achievement)

Assessment for learning

- The balance between planning for teacher questioning and being flexible enough to listen to and respond to different ideas is significant in lessons such as these. You will need to think about the types of questions that are asking the children to move their thinking on: Why did Prospero react the way he did? Did you expect Ferdinand and Miranda to fall in love? How do you think Ariel feels? What might happen to the young couple now? What do you think the ending of the play will be like?

Assessment at the point of learning
- The opportunity to watch and listen to children you know well, with a new and challenging text, is an ideal time for the teacher to move with the flow of learning; being ready to pounce on that exciting or insightful comment can be a way of harnessing learning and pushing the children to new realms of thinking. However, this does not happen without careful planning of the structure of the lesson and a good understanding of how teacher questioning is linked to better critical reading.

Assessment of learning
- The reflection on this lesson is imperative if you are going to get the pitch of the next lesson right. Not only will valuable learning be lost if there is no meaningful link between lessons but, more importantly, the pace and engagement levels will fade. Ensure that you know how the children have coped with the plot developments and the new interactions between characters. How have they responded to the language? Is now the time to spend some time experimenting with just a few segments to consolidate progress from this lesson?

Challenges

- The challenge in 'doing' Shakespeare includes the archaic language and forgetting that some of the complexities of plot were never intended to be read, but to be seen enacted on stage. The main premise is that the teacher understands this at the outset and looks to embrace both of these challenges with a creative, active and collaborative approach to text, exploring the wonderful stories within.

Application of learning

Links to other areas of the curriculum
As a starting point, it should be emphasised that this play was intended to be seen, and that a playful, dramatic approach will give the children the best experience. There are obvious cross-curricular links to history when focusing on a Shakespearean text: the opportunity for an exploration into the age in which the play was written, the playwright and his life, London and the theatre, the views of the Church or the monarch. Likewise, a play such as *The Tempest* will lend itself to exploring the ideas of a storm at sea, associated art and music, or the geography of the island itself. There will be much creativity and excitement in making these links and immersing learning within the world of this 'uninhabited island'.

Next lesson

Following on from the lesson above, give children the opportunity to do some writing within this creative context. You can set up the classroom to focus on the four characters in the middle of the room and ask what type of text we could place in it. Ideas might include a diary entry from Ferdinand on believing his father to be dead, a spell written by Prospero to conjure up a storm, a love letter or poem by Miranda, a magical wish for freedom by Ariel. The children will have to suspend their disbelief in terms of text (pens and paper) suddenly appearing in the scene, but it is an excellent way to contextualise writing and capture the deeper reading comprehension which will have gone on.

The 'placing the text' activity is best done in pairs with the children folding an extra piece of paper and putting their names on it. They then carefully place their 'text' into the still image in the centre of the room. The sculpture then comes to life with accompanied music, chooses and opens pieces of paper one by one. As pairs notice theirs being opened or picked up, they read their text. The whole activity is a dramatic sequence to music and should not be interrupted by comments or teacher interventions.

Learning outcomes review

After the planning, teaching and reflection on the learning, you should now have a greater understanding of how drama activities and collaborative learning can enhance the engagement and critical reading experience. The planned use of segments of text and teacher questions should have highlighted ways of working with Shakespeare which will lead to opening up differing interpretations within the classroom and effective, meaningful creative writing responses.

Further reading

Bunyan, P and Moore, R (2005) *NATE Drama Packs: Introduction Including Macbeth.* Sheffield: NATE.

A useful introduction to the pedagogy behind drama strategies in the English classroom and helpful schemes of work with resources to support. Transferable ideas for dealing with a range of texts.

Gibson, R (1998) *Teaching Shakespeare.* Cambridge: Cambridge University Press.

A handbook for teachers with a clear exploration of the pedagogy underpinning approaches to teaching Shakespeare. A wide range of strategies and practical ideas for a range of Shakespearean texts.

Royal Shakespeare Company (2010) *The RSC Shakespeare Toolkit for Teachers.* London: Methuen Drama.

A practical toolkit for planning to teach Shakespeare at Key Stage 2 and Key Stage 3.

References

Alexander, R (2004) *Towards Dialogic Teaching: Rethinking Classroom Talk*. York: Dialogos UK.

Boyd, M (2010) in Royal Shakespeare Company (2010) *The RSC Shakespeare Toolkit for Teachers*. London: Methuen Drama.

Department for Education (DfE) (2013) *The National Curriculum in England: Framework Document*. London: DfE.

Gibson, R (1998) *Teaching Shakespeare.* Cambridge: Cambridge University Press.

Shakespeare, W (1989 edn.) *The Tempest. The Arden Shakespeare*. London: Routledge.

Tennent, W (2015) *Understanding Reading Comprehension: Processes and Practices.* London: Sage.

Yandell, J and Franks, A (2014) Approaching Shakespeare, in Davison, J and Daly, C (eds.) *Learning to Teach English in the Secondary School*. London: Routledge.

Chapter 12

Year 6: Analysing pre-twentieth century literature

Learning outcomes

Pre-twentieth century literature can sometimes be eluded in the primary classroom due to the challenging nature of some of the language or the perception that the children will cover this at secondary school. This chapter considers how we can use pre-twentieth century fiction to continue to stimulate an active interest in reading and understanding the world around us. It will suggest ways of reading the text and further improving critical reading, while considering how these skills lead us to teaching writing more effectively.

This chapter will allow you to achieve the following outcomes:

- know how to sustain engagement and enjoyment of reading more challenging texts;
- understand how to develop deeper analysis of texts;
- develop teaching strategies that will facilitate enhanced creative writing sequences.

Teachers' Standards

Working through this chapter will help you meet the following standards:

1. Set high expectations which inspire, motivate and challenge pupils.
2. Promote good progress and outcomes by pupils.
3. Demonstrate good subject and curriculum knowledge.
4. Plan and teach well-structured lessons.
5. Adapt teaching to respond to the strengths and needs of all pupils.

Links to the National Curriculum

Years 5 and 6 programme of study

READING – Comprehension

Pupils should be taught to:

- maintain positive attitudes to reading and understanding what they read by:

  - ✓ continuing to read and discuss an increasingly wide range of fiction, poetry, plays, non-fiction and reference books or textbooks
  - ✓ increasing their familiarity with a wide range of books, including myths, legends, and traditional stories, modern fiction, fiction from our literary heritage, and books from their cultures and traditions
  - ✓ identifying and discussing themes and conventions in and across a wide range of writing
  - ✓ making comparisons within and across books

- understand what they read by:

  - ✓ checking that the book makes sense to them, discussing their understanding and exploring the meaning of words in context
  - ✓ asking questions to improve their understanding
  - ✓ drawing inferences such as inferring characters' feelings, thoughts and motives from their actions, and justifying inferences with evidence
  - ✓ predicting what might happen from details stated and implied
  - ✓ summarising the main ideas drawn from more than one paragraph, identifying key details that support the main ideas
  - ✓ identifying how language, structure and presentation contribute to meaning

- discuss and evaluate how authors use language, including figurative language, considering the impact on the reader
- participate in discussions about books that are read to them and those they can read for themselves, building on their own and others' ideas and challenging views courteously
- explain and discuss their understanding of what they have read
- provide reasoned justifications for their views.

(DfE, 2013)

Key focus: Teaching comprehension of challenging texts and critical literacy

Activity

Think about a text that you encountered at school which was a challenge. What made it more difficult? Was it a genre that you were unfamiliar with or did not like? Was the language more

(Continued)

(Continued)

difficult? Was the language archaic and therefore impenetrable? How did you overcome these challenges? To what extent did the teaching help you?

Now think about a challenging text that you have taught in the past. How have you considered hooking the children into the text? What types of teaching strategies helped you to overcome the difficulties in language or themes?

The research into teaching reading comprehension is vast and indeed many of the strategies and theorists have been referred to in this book. In this chapter, we will be considering the use of visualisation with older children as a means to finding a way into a difficult text. It is the increasing exposure to more challenging texts and developing the children's *critical* reading which sometimes creates a tension between this and continuing to develop their comprehension skills.

Park (2012) suggests that the strategy of visualisation can be used not only to teach comprehension of text but also to develop critical literacy. He defines critical literacy in two ways: the ability to understand how and why the text was written, and understanding the world/society in which we live. As the children become more competent readers with age and ability, we should not be deterred from explicitly teaching comprehension skills. The density and complexity of the new texts in front of them will still require explicit teaching of how to comprehend texts. This may mean revisiting some of the active reading strategies, like visualisation, but we will be re-purposing them to suit the demands of more challenging texts. The continuity of explicit use and teaching of them will not only provide appropriate scaffolding for children, but it will also give them a sense of security as they face a text which feels 'different'. Likewise, the conversations we have about these visualisations will be scaffolding the critical talk about text that will move children into a more analytical phase of their reading.

Park goes on to emphasise the need for talk *during* and *after* reading to make sense of meanings (2012). Once again, this prompts us to consider how we prepare children for accessing and enjoying more difficult texts. The collaborative approaches in reading, to which they are now accustomed, continue to be paramount in supporting them through new phases in text complexity. Managing our reading classrooms to facilitate meaningful talk about text can ensure that children are engaged in thoughtful conversations about their reading.

Collaborative learning

Rojas-Drummond *et al.* (2014) found that regular and structured opportunities to work collaboratively through reading comprehension activities resulted in improved levels of understanding and confidence with texts. However, while setting up classroom tasks which focus on collaborative approaches to text may be worthwhile, it is the quality of the talk that takes place that will determine the positive impact on learning. As Alexander (2004) asserts, talk that takes place in classrooms can be off task, un-cooperative and lacking in any real learning focus. Progression in children's ability to engage in exploratory talk will require focused planning and teaching. This will enable them to be able to use this as a means to tackle more challenging texts.

Exploratory talk

The lesson outlined below relies on the prerequisite of children having been taught how to engage in more productive talk for learning. The depth and richness of their exchanges afforded by exploratory talk (Mercer and Dawes, 2008) can enable them to uncover new meanings and look to read texts more critically. It is imperative, therefore, that this is part of their toolkit at this stage in their reading development, particularly if they are going to be able to cope with more challenging texts.

The teaching and learning strategies discussed here, in relation to one or two lessons, will require a holistic approach to teaching reading comprehension. It is the careful planning and teaching of reading strategies, linked to real opportunities to reflect, which will enlighten the children in their quest for understanding and meaning. As asserted by Mercer and Littleton (2007), the explicit teaching and metacognitive reflection on these processes will enable them to become competent and self-regulated readers who are ready to delve into challenging texts.

Teaching your class: Year 6

The text chosen here is the opening chapter of *Great Expectations* by Charles Dickens. There are a number of Victorian novels that will lend themselves to this age range in terms of setting, character and action. *Oliver Twist* is another Dickens novel which is appealing to this age range and looking at film versions provides excellent opportunities for comparison of interpretation. The challenge of the whole text can be minimised by looking at opening chapters and comparing them across a number of novels, or choosing one novel and planning ways of managing the size of the text. This might be through well-chosen extracts alongside an abridged version, not forgetting the wealth of film interpretations, which are excellent for comparative studies and worthy of literary study in their own right. An alternative text is *The Red Room* by H.G. Wells, a gothic short story, or *The Monkey's Paw* by W.W. Jacobs (first published in 1902).

Context

The children in this Year 6 class have considered themes, characters and plot in a range of fiction texts. They are confident in their understanding of what it means to infer and deduce and have explored different ways of doing this with their teacher. They have looked at some images relating to the late 1800s and have begun to make inferences about the times and the pervading culture. These visual stimuli might relate to the rural or urban deprivation of the time or the isolation of the Fens. This provides a suitable hook for understanding prior to the reading. In responding to their reading, they understand that they can retrieve elements of text which will help them to explain their opinions about character, plot or theme.

Learning objectives

- To infer how Pip and Magwitch felt in Chapter 1.

- To deduce a picture of the setting and link this to the atmosphere.

- To be able to explain how Dickens used language to convey these feelings and the atmosphere.

Commentary

The objectives outlined here will utilise the reading skills built up over a period of time by applying them to a more challenging text. The familiarity will lie in the concepts of inferring ideas related to character and deducing information within fiction text to create a picture of the setting. This will also link to previous preparatory work when the children revisited visual literacy techniques to zoom in and out on a picture (with teacher guidance) in order to consider different readings of a text. The visual stimuli will have served to support the different historical and/or geographical contexts present in Chapter 1 of this novel. The scaffolded approach to reading the text will support children's confidence in applying their understanding of the writer's craft to this text to illuminate a more critical reading.

Introduction to the lesson

Tell the children that you are going to read them a piece of text from the opening to a story. Ask them to close their eyes on the first reading and to imagine what they can see. Read the segment of Chapter 1 which begins, *Ours was the marsh country ...* to *and beginning to cry, was Pip.* Now, read the extract again and ask them to sketch what they can see in their mind's eye on their mini whiteboards. Tell them that on the third and final reading, they can add to the sketch by noting any words or phrases they think are important in setting the scene. Some of these words may be unfamiliar but this should not deter them from incorporating them in their record.

After they have done this, give them the opportunity in pairs to discuss and compare their 'pictures' of the opening scene in the chapter. Prompt them with questions for each other such as:

- Why did you draw that?

- How does that word link to your picture?

- Do our pictures look the same?

- How are our pictures different?

Ensure that all pairs are confident in collaborating in this activity. End the introduction by drawing together some key features of the talk you have heard as you circulated the room, which you can feed back to the class in terms of what the reader has learnt so far. This will also be an opportunity to pick up on any new or unusual words that the children have noticed.

Commentary

Children will have learnt about active reading skills and that visualisation is one of the ways of connecting with text (Ahmandi and Ismail, 2012; Manning, 2002; Park, 2012). It is important that the teacher facilitates the opportunity to do this regularly, and that it is emphasised that this skill will support the children when approaching new, challenging texts. Developing this skill over time in a collaborative learning environment will support the children in steadily building on their reading competencies towards independence and being good readers (Brown, 2008).

This activity not only provides the space to do this, but the follow-up questions also ensure that the children are focusing on the skills they have used to undertake the task. How they arrived at their picture/understanding and how this might be different to someone else's view is a significant part of the learning process when facing challenging texts. Over time, this will enable them to build their confidence and approach texts with an open mind.

Main lesson

Introduction

Have a copy of the rest of the chapter for each child, from *Hold your noise!* until the end. Depending on the ability of the class, this may be edited for some children. Read the rest of the chapter to the children, asking them to shut their eyes as they listen. Remind them that there might be some new or unusual vocabulary but that this does not matter at this stage. They are to focus on what they do understand; what the man is asking the young boy to do and how this makes them feel.

At the end of the reading, ask them to share their initial response to the text with their talk partner. How do they feel about these characters? What is happening in this extract?

Now set up a group activity for which you will have pre-prepared segments of the chapter on each table. There should be a copy of the rest of the chapter on A3 paper and parts highlighted for children to focus on. Accompanying this, they should be given a question to consider which encourages them to interrogate the text to arrive at a comprehension of either plot, characterisation or setting. This will be done using their investigative reading skills and working collaboratively at finding a shared meaning and co-constructing an interpretation.

This part of the text lends itself to the four parts outlined below.

1. *Hold your noise!* to … *keep myself from crying.*

2. … *keep myself from crying* to *He tilted me again.*

3. *He tilted me again* to *Now what do you say?*

4. *Now what do you say?* to *or the tide was in.*

Remind the children of skimming text to gain an overview or gist of what is happening and that they can look at their group's question to then scan the text for clues. Ask them what other reading skills they will be using now – i.e. questioning the text, inferring, deducing and predicting. It is important to keep these skills explicit and prominent even with competent readers at the stage when they are encountering more difficult texts. It tells the children that they are building on previous experience, and that they can transfer their reading skills to new and challenging texts as they get older and prepare for Key Stage 3.

Questions for the four parts of the chapter could include:

1. Can you build up a picture of the man and how he behaves? What shocks Pip? How does Pip feel?

2. What has he got to do for the man? Why do you think the man needs these things?

3. How does the man in the story make you feel? What does he say to scare Pip some more?

4. Can you describe what Pip sees as the man leaves him? How does the setting make you feel as a reader?

The children should be given time to interrogate the text using highlighters or pens to make notes on the text if it helps them to make sense of their reading and organise their ideas. This will be an opportunity for the teacher to circulate the room and listen to conversations about the reading, avoiding intervening but watching to see how they are responding to the challenge.

The children should then be brought back together to share their questions and responses. In doing so, the teacher can challenge where appropriate and ask children to cite parts of the text that helped them to uncover some new meanings.

Commentary

Underpinning these activities is an understanding that children can benefit from collaborative learning in order to work on a co-constructed interpretation of text. Planning for learning activities which facilitate peer collaboration guides the children towards considering different, critical responses to text (Rojas-Drummond et al., 2014). By giving them a clear focus through the questions and a manageable amount of text to deal with, the teacher is setting some parameters to support the fact that they are moving towards increasingly challenging texts. The scaffolds and removal of teacher-directed talk at this point allows the children to enter into dialogue to investigate the text. Through previous learning the children should now be used to exploratory talk, which will be another implicit support for them when inferring meaning from nineteenth century text. This activity will give the children the opportunity to engage critically with the ideas in the text and to share a consensus on meaning (Mercer, 2000).

It will be important for the teacher to guide the children when they are giving feedback – they will need to be questioned about the thinking behind their comprehension of the text and what it was about the shared discussions that enabled them to make sense of what they read. There will be a balance between enjoying the personal responses to the literary text and lifting the dialogue to a metacognitive level, whereby the children are able to trace the reading process and therefore learn from the experience as a lifelong reader. At this point, as noted by Mercer and Littleton (2007), there may be children who will revisit their thoughts and change their ideas – a wonderful opportunity to talk about what it means to be a reader.

Plenary

Tell the children that you are going to read the final paragraph from this chapter. While they are listening to you, they need to listen out for three things that add to their personal picture of this part of the story. They can use their mini whiteboards to record their ideas; this might be three words, phrases or a quick sketch.

Ask the children to hold up their responses after a few minutes so that you can see them all. Ask two or three children to show their boards and explain what is on them.

You may wish to ask more able children for an extra challenge, also allowing others to hear a good explanation modelled for them. Alternatively, you might ask children who have excelled in this particular approach in order to make explicit to them what reading skills they have used during the lesson.

Commentary

By asking the children to visualise again at the end of the lesson, the teacher will be reiterating the skill they used earlier. Having been immersed in the text and having had the opportunity to collaborate in their investigations of the text, the children are now given the opportunity to try and do this independently. There is still no pressure to conform to one reading of the text and the teacher's response to individuals at the end should emphasise this.

Assessment (measuring achievement)

Assessment for learning

- Using your knowledge of children's abilities in reading and exploratory talk will be significant in setting up appropriate groups for the main task. This will be an opportunity to differentiate through groups, text or questions. Likewise, in some instances, it will be appropriate to mix children to allow for good peer modelling or additional scaffolding for some children.

- Planning your teacher questions for parts of the lesson where there is feedback will help you to challenge and prompt where necessary.

Assessment at the point of learning

- While not engaging in the group discussion, the teacher should use this time as a valuable opportunity to monitor progress and understanding. Intervention may be necessary, but the aim is to promote peer support and exploration. For more able groups, the teacher can use sticky notes to add questions to the table. This can add a sense of pace and challenge for able children.

Assessment of learning

- Teacher reflections on the learning that has taken place will be significant in the steps for planning ahead. However, there should be no formal summative assessment at this point as the teacher will want to continue to set up explorative learning activities to build on the skills and to enjoy the text. The next lesson's activity with a storyboard could be used as a diagnostic tool to measure comprehension and this could be explained to children during the instructions to give credence to the explanations you are seeking about their choice of camera angle.

Challenges

- The challenge to a teacher promoting a range of literary texts is that the children may have preconceptions about the text, the author or the time in which it was written. Keeping reading active and collaborative as children are exposed to increasingly difficult texts is pivotal in keeping the parameters of their reading experiences open. Planning carefully for this has to be at the heart of reading progression for older children. The teacher's attitude towards text becomes increasingly significant for young people, likewise the discussion about being a 'reader'. How the teacher prepares a reading of a complex text is also important; a poor delivery can make a difference to the children's first impression of a text and should not be underestimated. As a teacher, how do you read this extract to convey the tension and the sense of foreboding?

Application of learning

Links to other areas of the curriculum

There are numerous links to other areas of the curriculum with this text, not least, drama, history, citizenship and personal, social and health education. Likewise, the ability to embrace a challenging text and to make sense of it using a toolkit of tried and tested strategies will be of benefit when dealing with a range of texts across the curriculum. The more explicit the teacher commentary, the greater the transferral of skills to other areas.

Next lesson

In the next lesson, split the groups into pairs and provide them with a storyboard grid with no more than five boxes with accompanying boxes for captions. Tell them that you are not worried about their artistic ability in this activity (stick people will suffice), but you are interested in their interpretation of the text. They are going to work in role as a film director on the short piece of text they explored in the last lesson. They must choose how to convey the most significant aspects of the plot, setting or characterisation through the type of camera angle or shot. They will have worked on these terms before and are now using this terminology in order to show that they have a personal response to this text. Will there be a close-up of Magwitch's face to convey the sinister feel to the text? Or a picture of him holding Pip upside down to show the physical power he has over Pip? Is the graveyard scene significant in conveying an atmosphere to the reader? The focus should be on what they are hoping to convey in each box.

Children should fill in the captions with a sentence to capture the scene, and through this they should try to explain what it is that they hope to convey. For example, a medium shot of Magwitch holding Pip upside down to allow a view of the graveyard, which adds to the sinister feel of the meeting. In this way, they are justifying their ideas and still involved in the collaborative approach to support their exploration. Sharing these with the rest of the group will be of interest, to revisit the idea of close reading with a personal response alongside the varied readings from other people.

Learning outcomes review

You have now worked through familiar teaching and learning strategies for reading comprehension and considered how these can best be applied to more challenging texts. The opportunity to collaborate and enter into exploratory talk is still of paramount importance to young readers at this stage of their reading journey. We have looked at how these strategies can be incorporated into active reading sessions that dwell on personal and co-constructed meanings and interpretations of text. As ever, keeping the teacher commentary explicit and signposting skills will enable the children to learn not only about Pip and the scary, escaped convict, but also how they can have the confidence to explore and grapple with text to make sense of it. As well as an enjoyable experience in its own right, we are preparing them for Key Stage 3 and the delights of other literary explorations.

Further reading

Kispal, A (2008) *Effective Teaching of Inference Skills for Reading: Literature Review.* National Foundation for Educational Research. Research Report DCSF-RR031.

A useful overview of teaching inference at Key Stages 2 and 3. A summary of research and strategies for the classroom.

References

Ahmandi, M and Ismail, H (2012) Reciprocal teaching strategy as an important factor of improving reading comprehension. *Journal of Studies in Education*, 2 (4).

Alexander, R (2004) *Towards Dialogic Teaching: Rethinking Classroom Talk*. York: Dialogos UK.

Brown, R (2008) The road not yet taken: a transactional strategies approach to comprehension instruction. *The Reading Teacher*, 61 (7): 538–47.

Department for Education (DfE) (2013) *The National Curriculum in England: Framework Document*. London: DfE.

Dickens, C (1985 edn.) *Great Expectations*. London: Penguin Classics.

Manning, M (2002) Visualizing when reading. *Teaching pre K-8*, Early Years Inc. 32 (8): 89.

Mercer, N (2000) *Words and Minds: How We Use Language to Think Together*. London: Routledge.

Mercer, N and Dawes, L (2008) The value of exploratory talk, in Mercer, N and Hodgkinson, S (eds.) *Exploring Talk in School*. London: Sage.

Mercer, N and Littleton, K (2007) *Dialogue and the Development of Children's Thinking: A Socio Cultural Approach*. London: Routledge.

Park, J (2012) A different kind of reading instruction: using visualisation to bridge reading comprehension and critical literacy. *Journal of Adolescent and Adult Literacy*, 55 (7): 629.

Rojas-Drummond, S, Mazon, N, Littleton, K and Velez, M (2014) Developing reading comprehension through collaborative learning. *Journal of Research in Reading*, 37 (2): 138–58.

Chapter 13

Moving on: Reading for pleasure

Learning outcomes

This chapter will allow you to achieve the following outcomes:

- understand the importance of the learning environment when teaching reading comprehension;
- understand how you might adapt the lesson examples in previous chapters to suit the needs of your learners;
- know how to promote reading for pleasure across the school and within your own classroom.

Teachers' Standards

Working through this chapter will help you meet the following standards:

3. Demonstrate good subject and curriculum knowledge.
4. Plan and teach well-structured lessons.
5. Adapt teaching to respond to the strengths and needs of all pupils.

Introduction

The lesson examples outlined in the previous chapters have, at their heart, purposeful reading for enjoyment. They have been written in order to demonstrate how children can develop their reading comprehension skills in a variety of ways, taking into account children's prior knowledge and attainment. Each chapter has a key pedagogical focus that will help teach children the necessary skills to access and enjoy a variety of texts. We have drawn from an extensive literature base in order to outline best practice and consider the key pedagogical approaches that lead to success in reading comprehension. A significant feature of the lesson plans is the accompanying commentary, which serves to exemplify best practice and guide you to adapt the lesson so that it is successful for you and your class.

The lessons are not intended to cover the whole of the reading curriculum but outline ways in which you can teach skills. Adapting the lessons to suit the needs of your learners will ensure that you personalise learning effectively. We consider texts in their broadest form, ranging from oral stories to multimodal texts; these are designed to engage and enthuse the children in your class and develop a rich and varied reading environment.

Comprehension skills can be modelled and taught in a variety of ways; you do not have to wait for a timetabled guided reading session, although this in itself is a very valuable time for opening up discussions and dialogue that ensure children are actively engaging with the text. By teaching reading in a creative and engaging manner through employing key pedagogical approaches, your lessons will foster positive reading attitudes that will lead to lifelong readers (Horton *et al.*, 2013).

Activity

Consider your own reading journey: map out your life in terms of books and the memories associated with them. You might begin with a book that you remember reading as a child or indeed one that was read to you. Can you remember the emotions that you felt? It could go on to include examples from your school life, books read for exams, holiday novels read in the sun. How did you feel about these books and what do you think influenced your enjoyment of each? Have you had any negative experiences with reading? Why do you think this was?

Reflect upon what contributed to you becoming the reader that you are today.

Lifelong reading

A number of studies indicate attainment is higher in children who have a positive attitude towards reading (Clark and De Zoysa, 2011; Petscher, 2010; Twist *et al.*, 2007). However, the number of children reading for pleasure seems to be decreasing, as evidenced in international surveys such as the Progress in International Reading Literacy Study (PIRLS) and the Programme for International Student Assessment (PISA) study (PIRLS, 2006; OECD, 2009), and is highlighted by Clark and Rumbold (2006) in their overview for the National Literacy Trust. OFSTED recommended that schools implement whole-school policies around reading for pleasure in an attempt to address inconsistencies in children's engagement with reading (OFSTED, 2012); therefore, it is crucial that we develop a classroom environment that not only addresses reading for enjoyment, but actively promotes it.

A whole-school approach

Case study

Reading for pleasure remains a high priority for many schools, especially in light of statutory guidance from the government. This case study highlights results from an evaluation of a whole-school reading promotion plan implemented by a school comprising data collated from children and staff immediately prior to and following the implementation of the programme.

The programme consisted of reading promotion activities from the 'Lifelong Readers' project website (**www.lifelongreaders.org**), trialled in school to evaluate effectiveness and suitability, together with planned whole-school events in order to raise the profile of reading within the school and wider community, raise standards of attainment in reading, encourage a willingness to read for pleasure and to encourage confident, enthusiastic readers.

Three training workshops were carried out in school to develop the reading promotion plan and train teachers to use the reading promotion activities; activities were trialled in school and a reading promotion audit was completed and a reading promotion plan produced by the school.

Having discussed our own reading journeys and personal values about reading during the first workshop, the teachers described their ideal 'reading classroom', which included a welcoming environment, a variety of books and other reading materials, having displays on the walls that actively promoted reading, books on the teacher's desk, a 'book/author of the week' display; referring to the invisible ethos of the school together with the physical environment. There was a general consensus among the staff that reading was held in high regard as part of the underlying ethos of the school and was represented in all classrooms. The main areas to be addressed were: visibility of reading within the school, teachers as readers, suitability and use of the school library and reading events to promote reading for pleasure.

Indications from data collected following implementation of the plan suggest that the reading promotion activities delivered across the school were successful in raising the profile of reading and led to increased discussion in classrooms around books and authors. Reading recommendations, reading cafes and teacher/learner conferences contributed to building communities of readers and whole-school events including dressing up as a book character, extreme reading and author of the term increased the visibility of reading. The most significant impact was upon children reading at home and choosing to read during their free time and in the school holidays. In addition, results showed that more children were choosing to visit bookshops and libraries, indicating an upsurge in the enjoyment of reading. Furthermore, statutory tests taken in Year 2 demonstrated higher levels of attainment in reading.

The key challenges for the school centred on the monitoring of the reading initiatives and ensuring sustainability. However, all members of staff agreed that it was important to continue to foster this love of reading and continue the momentum that the project had generated. Key recommendations that were taken forward included the following:

- Involving children in the formulation of activities so as to build upon their interests.
- Reading promotion activities should be tailored to the needs of individual children and classes.
- Opportunities for older children to carry out reading promotion activities with younger children to enable them to be exposed to different texts and to share positive reading experiences should feature as part of school culture.
- Teachers need to be seen as readers within the context of the classroom and promote reading for pleasure within their spare time. Teachers were advised to read every day with the children and allow them to see you as the teacher reading a book that you find interesting.

From the case study, we can appreciate the benefits of a whole-school approach in promoting reading for pleasure and the results speak for themselves. By implementing initiatives such as reading challenges and 'book of the week', visibility of reading is raised across the school and children are more likely to participate in conversations around reading both at school and at home. The recommendations emphasise a level of child autonomy and collaboration in order to provide a successful reading approach in terms of engaging children in wider reading. Indeed, John Guthrie concluded that the classrooms that are most successful in engaging readers are those that provide opportunities for collaborative work where children have the opportunity to co-construct meaning (a feature of all the lessons exemplified in previous chapters); allow individual choice; and where teachers explicitly teach reading strategies (Guthrie *et al.*, 1996).

The reading environment

Teachers as readers

The classroom environment encompasses much more than the physical objects that furnish classrooms. Your classroom environment includes you as the teacher, a crucial element when looking at reading for pleasure. As you will have seen from the case study above, the role of the teacher in motivating and engaging children in reading can have a significant influence on attitudes. If we reflect on the research cited above, it is clear to see how this may consequently impact upon attainment in reading.

A year-long project, 'Teachers as readers: building communities of readers', found that practitioners were heavily reliant on a narrow canon of children's authors when teaching reading in school. The project encouraged teachers to extend their knowledge of children's authors, develop confidence in using literature in the classroom and increase the visibility of themselves as readers within the classroom

(Cremin *et al.*, 2009). Children need to see their teachers as role models for reading and feel confident to discuss their ideas and opinions with their teachers and peers. From the case study above, the data suggested that children did not always perceive their teachers to be readers and could not tell me whether their teacher enjoyed reading. However, when teachers were questioned as to what they felt, they were adamant in their belief that the children in their class knew that they loved reading. This apparent mismatch of perceptions fuelled a renewed effort to demonstrate teachers' love of reading. Activities were specifically introduced so as to address this area and included:

- teachers' favourite author display boards;

- leaving a novel on the desk so that children could see that teachers were engaged in their own reading;

- discussing favourite books with their class;

- employing 'stop and drop' activities, whereby at certain points in the day both children and teachers read from their current book for a period of time;

- teachers sharing their reading journeys.

This contributed significantly to children understanding that their teachers were also readers and provided an excellent role model in terms of reading for pleasure. You may need to consider how your class views you as a reader. Do you make this explicit? Are you able to make recommendations based on your knowledge of children's literature? Does your classroom environment lend itself to purposeful and informed discussion about books and reading?

The reading area

Activity

Take a large piece of paper and design your ideal reading classroom. What does it look like? What types of resources will you provide? What do the wall displays say about reading? Do you have a designated reading area? What does it look like?

This is a valuable activity as it encourages you to consider how best to promote reading within the classroom. The messages that you convey through your classroom design will influence children's engagement in and motivation to read. If we think back to Guthrie's suggestion as to what makes an effective reading environment (Guthrie *et al.*, 1996), a certain level of autonomy is necessary to enhance reading engagement. Do the children in your class have opportunities to choose their own reading material or are they restricted to choosing books from a prescribed book band? How do you guide and influence individual choice? Is your book area stocked with texts that you think your class should be reading or does it reflect their choices and interests? Have you ever considered asking children to provide their own wish lists when you are re-stocking your bookshelves? Their choices may surprise you.

By providing access to a reading area that contains diverse reading material, you will be promoting reading which in itself will lead to increased engagement, thus contributing to increased attainment. It may also be beneficial to consider how you utilise ebooks in the classroom and organise tablets and reading devices so that children have access to digital texts as well as book-based texts. An effectively designed book area that provides opportunities for children to engage in independent and collaborative reading is crucial when developing our reading environment (Lockwood, 2008; Reutzel and Fawson, 2004).

Parental engagement

Engaging with reading outside of school is another important factor in increasing attainment in reading. In a report published by the National Literacy Trust, it was revealed that *young people are more likely to be reading above the level expected for their age the more books they read outside of class* (Clark and De Zoysa, 2011, p7). This is also supported by evidence from international studies which suggest that regular reading outside of school leads to increased scores on reading assessments (PIRLS, 2006; OECD, 2009). Therefore, it is crucial that schools work with parents to foster positive links and to maintain communication with those who support children's reading at home. In his book, *Promoting Reading for Pleasure in the Primary School*, Michael Lockwood states:

> *The best way parents can help the teacher, usually, is by encouraging pleasure reading at home, by reading together with their children and talking about books read, rather than through trying to teach reading.*

> (Lockwood, 2008, p39)

Engaging parents may take the form of reading records and logs, which requires some sort of dialogue between home and school, usually with child input. This serves to highlight the importance of home reading and encourages interaction between parent and child when reading at home. However, if we want to truly promote reading for pleasure at home, parents should not perceive it to be a chore, hastily filling in the boxes of the reading record. Some of the most successful schools have parental engagement as an aim on their development plan and provide a wide range of activities and meetings to share expertise with parents. They spend time working with parents to secure positive reading habits for their children.

Case study

This primary school values reading for pleasure and is committed to engaging parents in sharing books and developing reading at home. Reading meetings begin in Reception, with parents being invited to attend a short meeting and a series of workshops where children share their own thoughts and views on reading. These are repeated as children move into different year groups, and each has a different focus. In Reception, parents are provided with guidance on how to share books and explore illustrations and picture books so that parent and child can have those rich conversations around narrative, character and setting as suggested in Chapter 3. The meeting in Year 2 focuses on developing comprehension skills and questioning techniques, with suggested reading lists on offer. As children move into Key Stage 2, the focus becomes more targeted; activities such as 'Dads reading' and reading challenges (including the National Literacy Trust's football challenge **www.literacytrust. org.uk/premier_league_reading_stars**) are central to home/school reading liaison, while Year 6 meetings centre on higher order skills and providing challenges for more able readers, together with recommendations for appropriate reading material. In addition, parents have opportunities to attend guided reading sessions in school so as to enhance their understanding of how reading is developed in school through observing teachers modelling reading for purpose and pleasure.

The school also provides many other activities and opportunities. For example:

- book quizzes for children and parents;
- book fairs;
- extreme reading competitions;
- bedtime reading sessions (parents are invited into school to share a story with their child over a hot chocolate);
- reading clubs;
- attendance at class assemblies where reading for pleasure is a central theme;
- reading challenges;
- competitions;
- visits from authors.

The case study above illustrates how you can encourage parents to become more involved in their child's reading and foster positive reading habits. Needless to say, attainment in reading was very high across the school.

Activity

Review this chapter and identify how you might construct a whole-school plan for promoting reading for pleasure. Choose three key aims you consider might be priorities and outline the ways in which you could implement them across a key stage or year group.

Learning outcomes review

By now, you should have an understanding of the importance of developing a strong school ethos to support children's reading for pleasure, using the learning environment to enhance this. You should also be aware of the importance of developing a consistent and engaging environment to support children's learning. You should be able to adapt and develop the lesson examples from previous chapters to support, extend and challenge children's thinking in terms of reading comprehension. The case studies offer a practical approach that outlines best practice and makes explicit the links between research and practice.

Useful websites

www.literacytrust.org.uk – a website which actively promotes reading for pleasure and brings together significant research and practice to improve children's reading.

www.readingforpleasure.org.uk – provides free resources to be used in educational settings.

www.lifelongreaders.org.uk – research from an international perspective, with practical activities designed to engage and motivate learners.

Further reading

Chambers, A (2011) *Tell Me: Children, Reading and Talk*. Stroud: Thimble Press.

Together with his website, **www.aidanchambers.co.uk/index.htm**, this book offers practitioner-based advice for developing and sustaining book conversations, allowing children to engage in effective dialogue which actively promotes reading comprehension.

DfES (2005) *Raising Standards in Reading: Achieving Children's Targets*. London: DfES.

This primary national strategy document, although archived, outlines key priorities for schools in terms of raising attainment in reading.

Hall, K (2003) *Listening to Stephen Read: Multiple Perspectives on Literacy*. Buckingham: OUP.

This book offers many perspectives on reading drawn from the responses of reading experts. It is steeped in rigorous research, which supports the teaching of reading using a variety of approaches.

References

Clark, C and De Zoysa, S (2011) *Mapping the Interrelationships of Reading Enjoyment, Attitudes, Behaviour and Attainment: An Exploratory Investigation*. London: National Literacy Trust.

Clark, C and Rumbold, K (2006) *Reading for Pleasure: A Research Overview*. London: The National Literacy Trust.

Cremin, T, Mottram, M, Collins, F, Powell, S and Safford, K (2009) Teachers as readers: building communities of readers. *Literacy*, 43 (1): 11–19.

Guthrie, JT, Van Meter, P, McCann, AD, Wigfield, A, Bennett, L, Punndstone, CC, Rice, ME, Faibisch, FM, Hunt, B and Mitchell, AM (1996) Growth of literacy engagement: changes in motivations and strategies during concept-oriented reading instruction. *Reading Research Quarterly*, 31: 306–32.

Horton, S, Sullivan, P and Robertson, C (2013) *Lifelong Readers: A European Reading Promotion Framework for Primary School Librarians, Educators and Administrators (LiRe)*. A report based on findings from England and Ireland. Cyprus: CARDET.

Lockwood, M (2008) *Promoting Reading for Pleasure in the Primary School*. London: Sage.

OFSTED (2012) *Moving English Forward*. London: OFSTED.

Organisation for Economic Co-operation and Development (2009) *PISA 2009 Results: Executive Summary*.

Petscher, Y (2010) A meta-analysis of the relationship between student attitudes towards reading and achievement in reading. *Journal of Research in Reading*, 33 (4): 335–55.

Progress in International Reading Literacy Study International Report (2006) Available at: **http://timssandpirls.bc.edu/pirls2006/intl_rpt.html**

Reutzel, DR and Fawson, PC (2004) *Your Classroom Library: New Ways to Give It More Teaching Power*. London: Scholastic.

Twist, L, Schagan, I and Hogson, C (2007) *Progress in International Reading Literacy Study (PIRLS): Readers and Reading National Report for England 2006*. Slough: NFER.

Index